Florida's Amazing

Silver River

One of Florida's Natural Wonders

Photographer/Author ~ Rick Bopp

FLORIDA'S AMAZING SILVER RIVER
One of Florida's Natural Wonders
Photos by Rick Bopp

CREATESPACE Softcover Edition

Printed in the United States of America

First Printing 2013

ISBN: 9781481898492

Printed and Kindle versions available at Amazon.com

Photographer and Author: Rick Bopp
For more information: rickbopp@gmail.com

Photos available at rickbopp.com

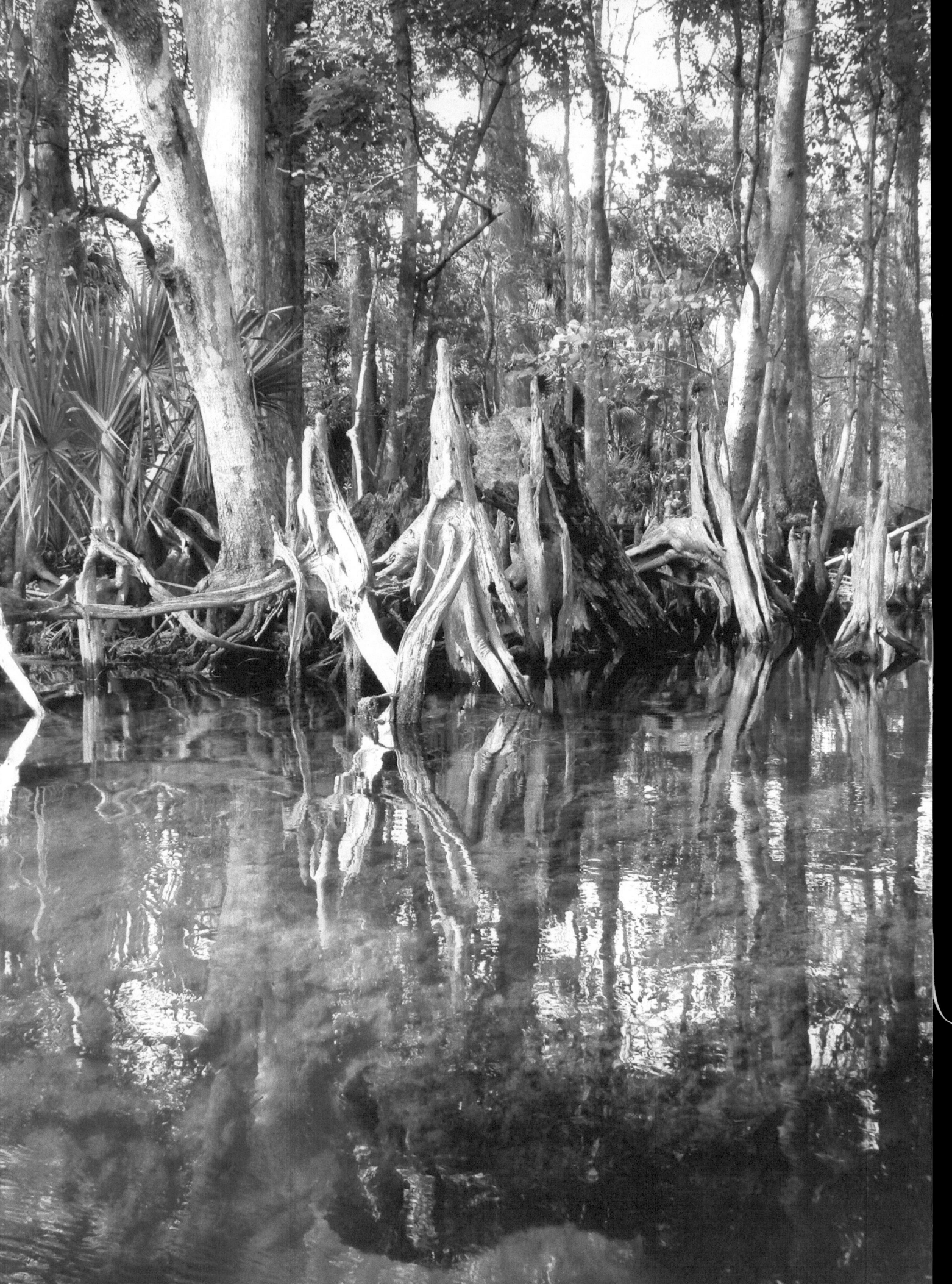

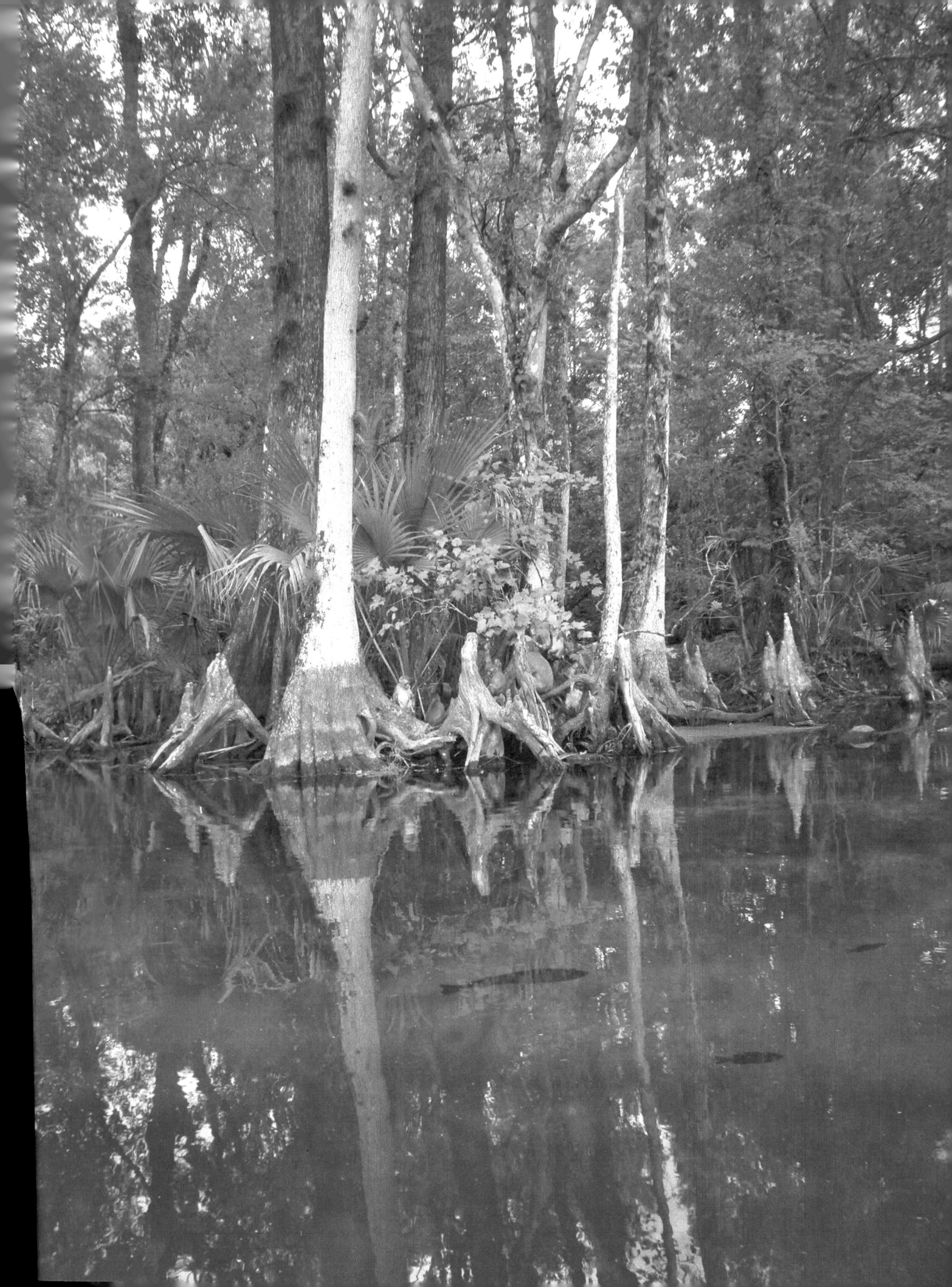

The *Silver River* watershed flowing through *Silver River State Park* is an amazing and pristine wetland of subtropical trees, fauna and wildlife that make it a virtual wonderland of nature.

The Silver Springs artesian well just east of *Ocala, Florida* is the headwater of the Silver River. It is one of the largest underground aquifer fed springs in the world. It pours forth from the earth continually, historically producing over half a billion gallons of sparkling fresh water each day!

One way that many people have viewed the massive spring is via glass bottom boat at *Silver Springs Nature Theme Park* off highway 40 on the east edge of the city of *Silver Springs, Florida.* The land surrounding Silver Springs Nature Theme Park land was purchased by the state of Florida's Board of Trustees of the Internal Improvement Trust Fund in 1993 in order to protect this natural wonder. Until presently, the park has been run by a private corporation. Some changes in this access to the spring head are developing at this time. It is scheduled to be managed by Silver River State Park beginning Oct. 1, 2013 as part of Florida's Park Service.

The rhesus monkeys that can be spotted along the riverbank have descended from a group of monkeys which were introduced as a park attraction in the 1930's. Many movies and television shows have been filmed in and along this amazing water world including the *Tarzan* movies featuring Johnny Weissmuller.

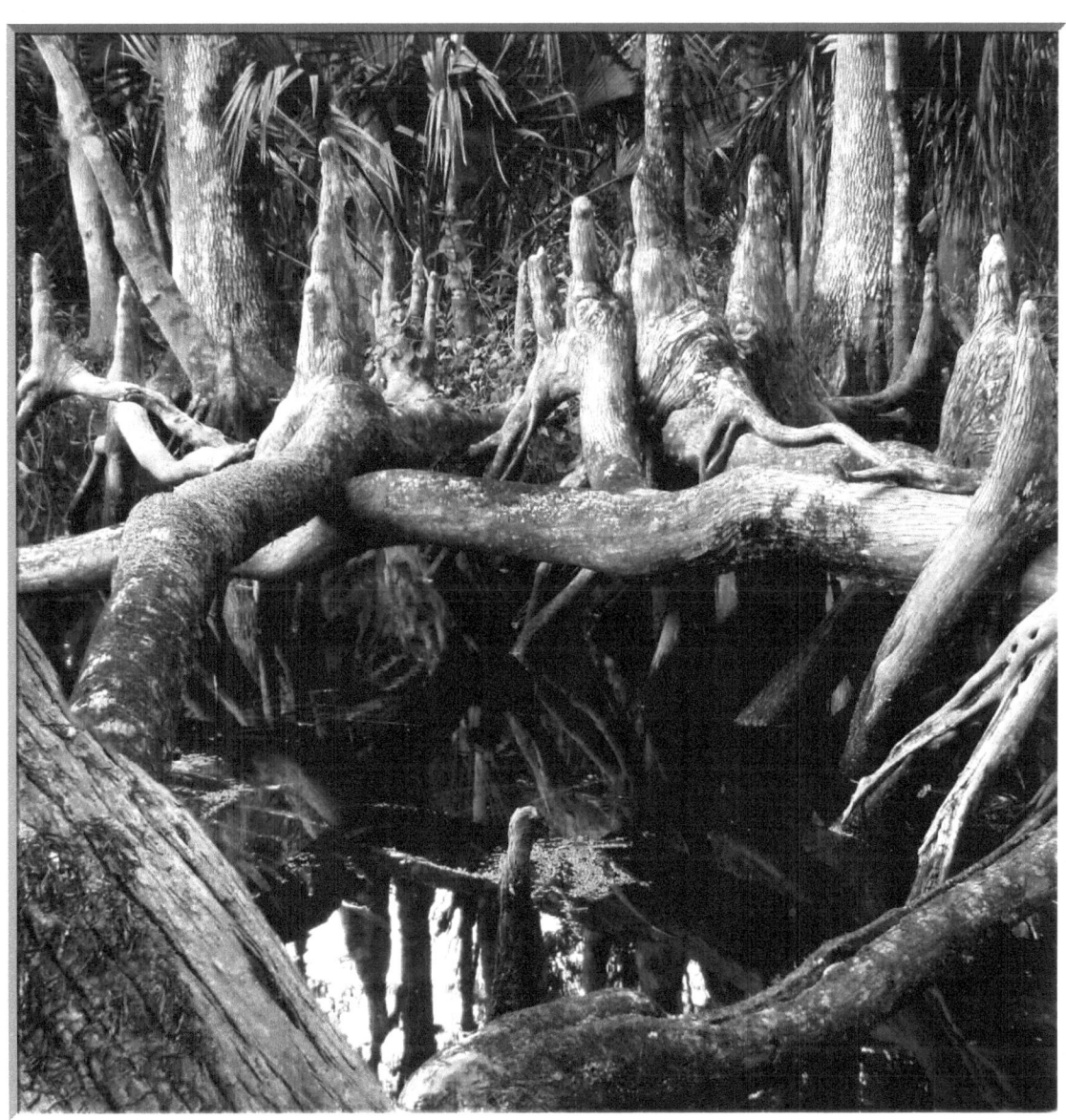

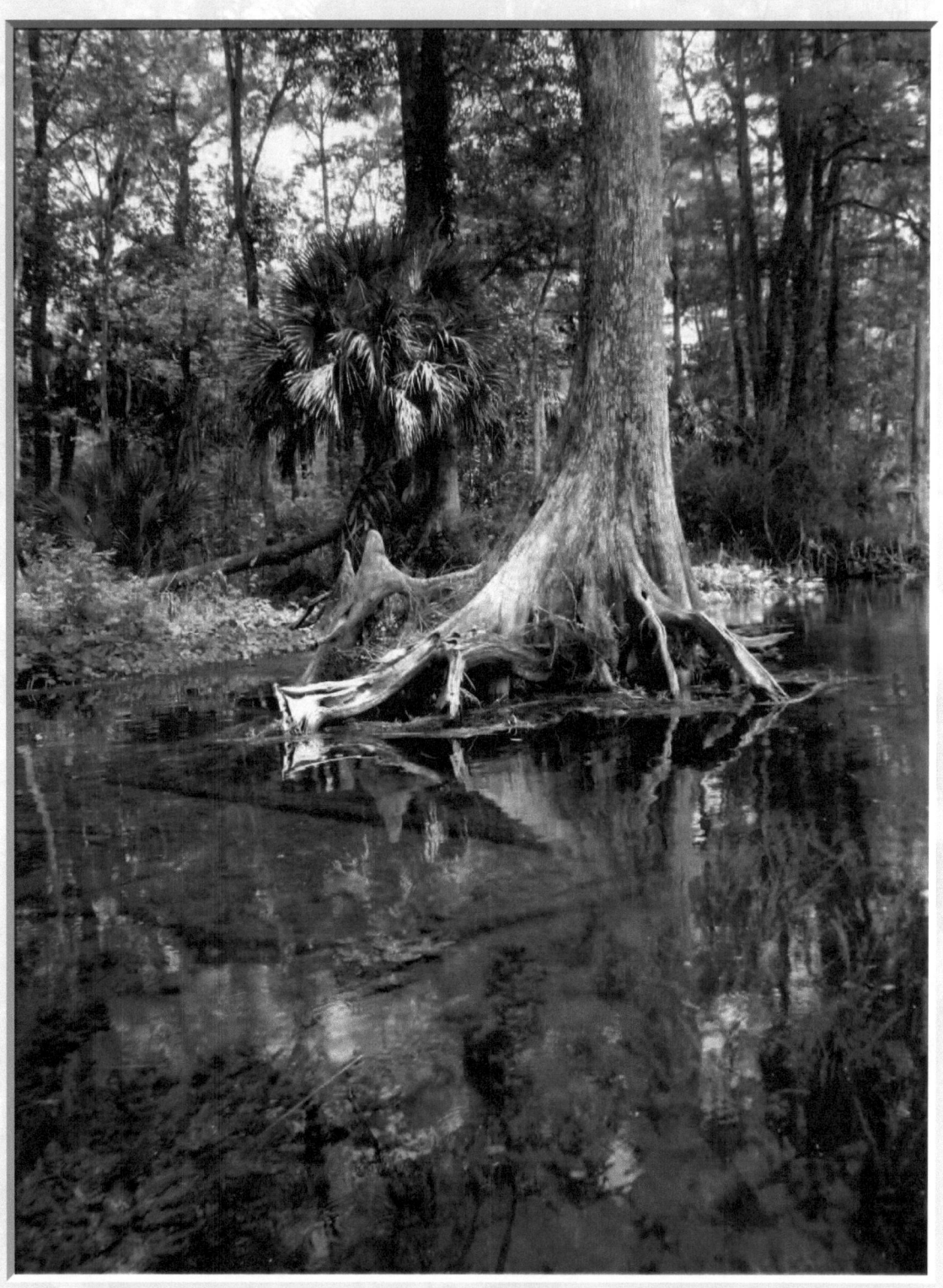

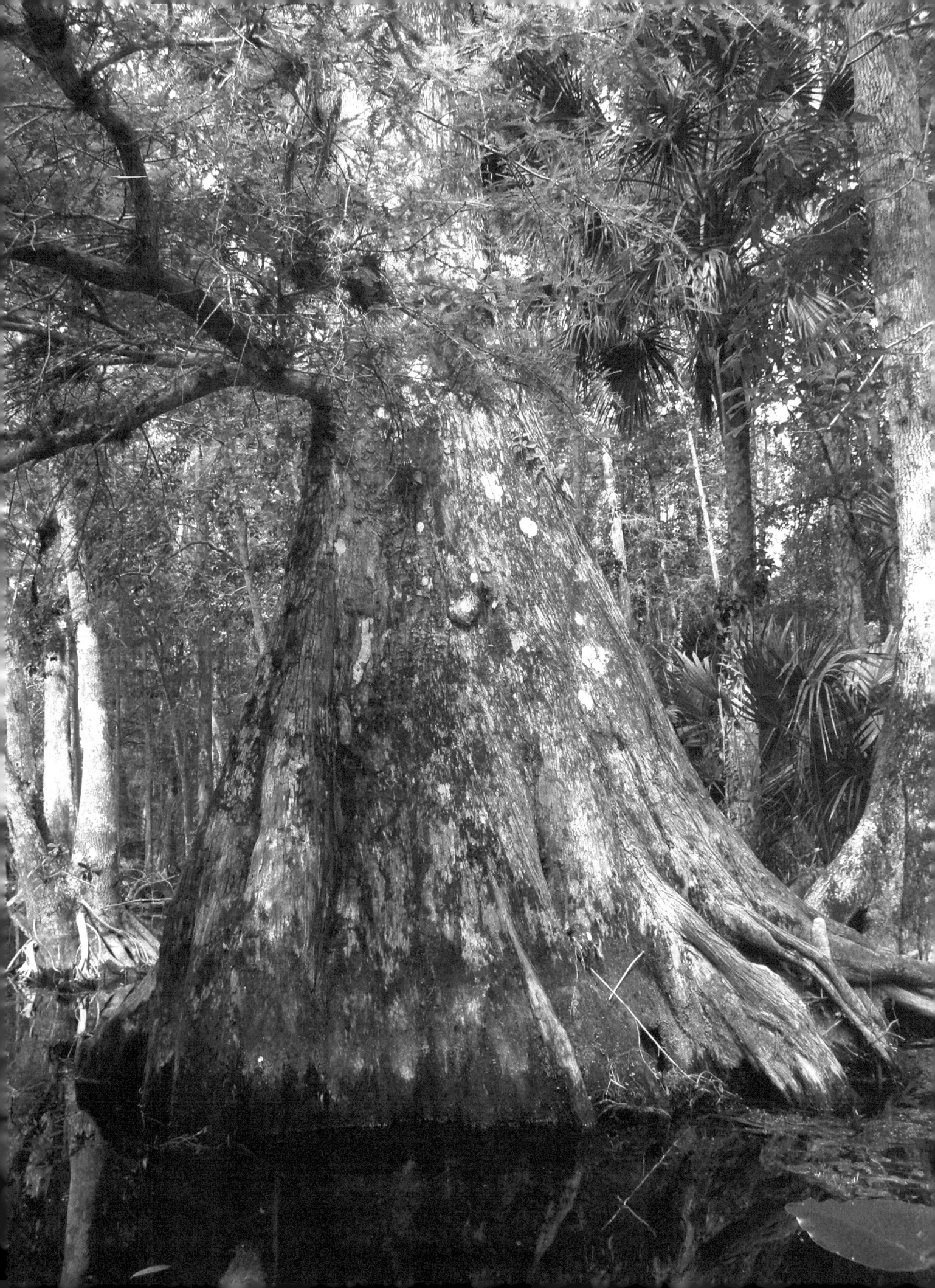

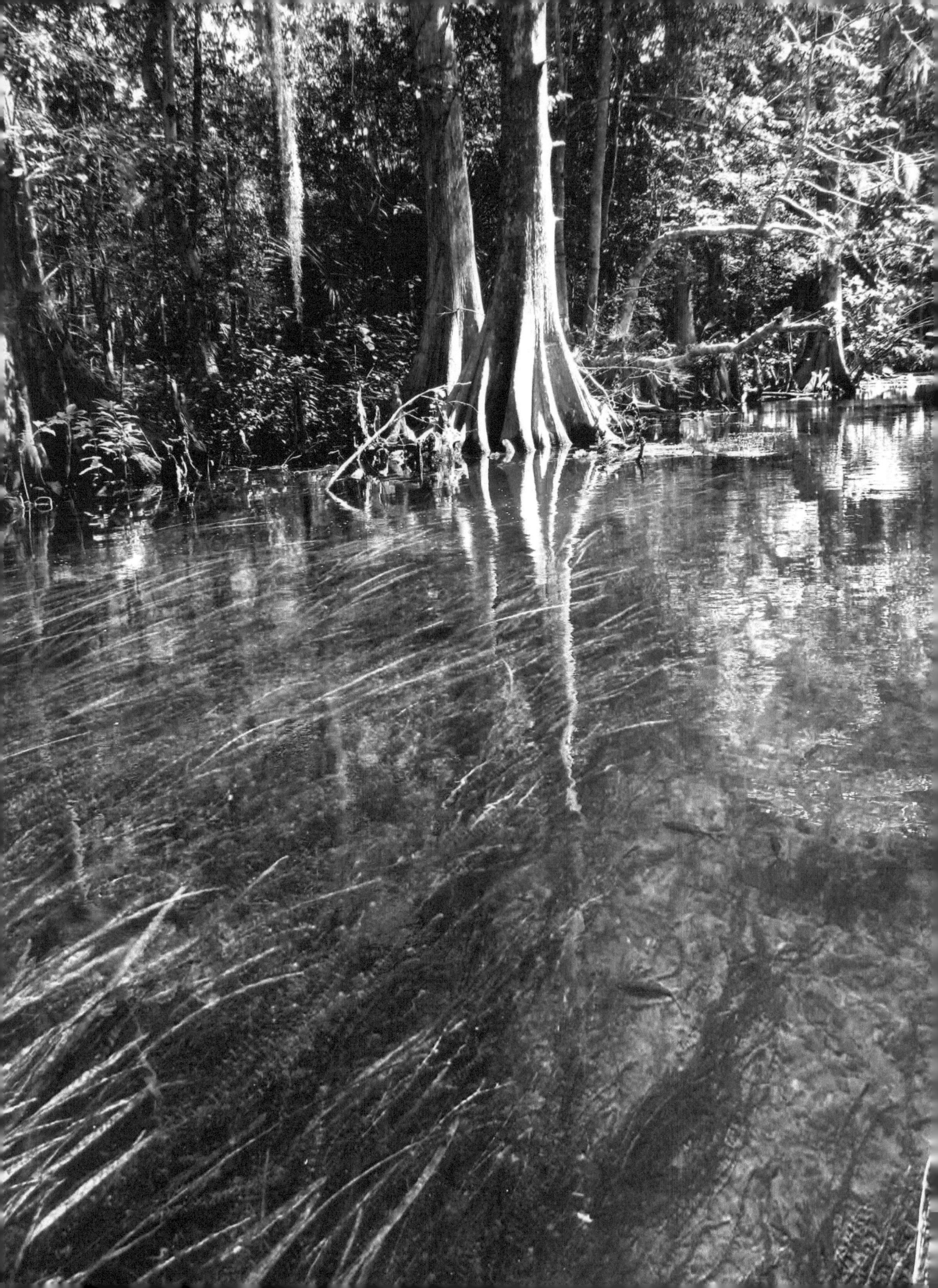

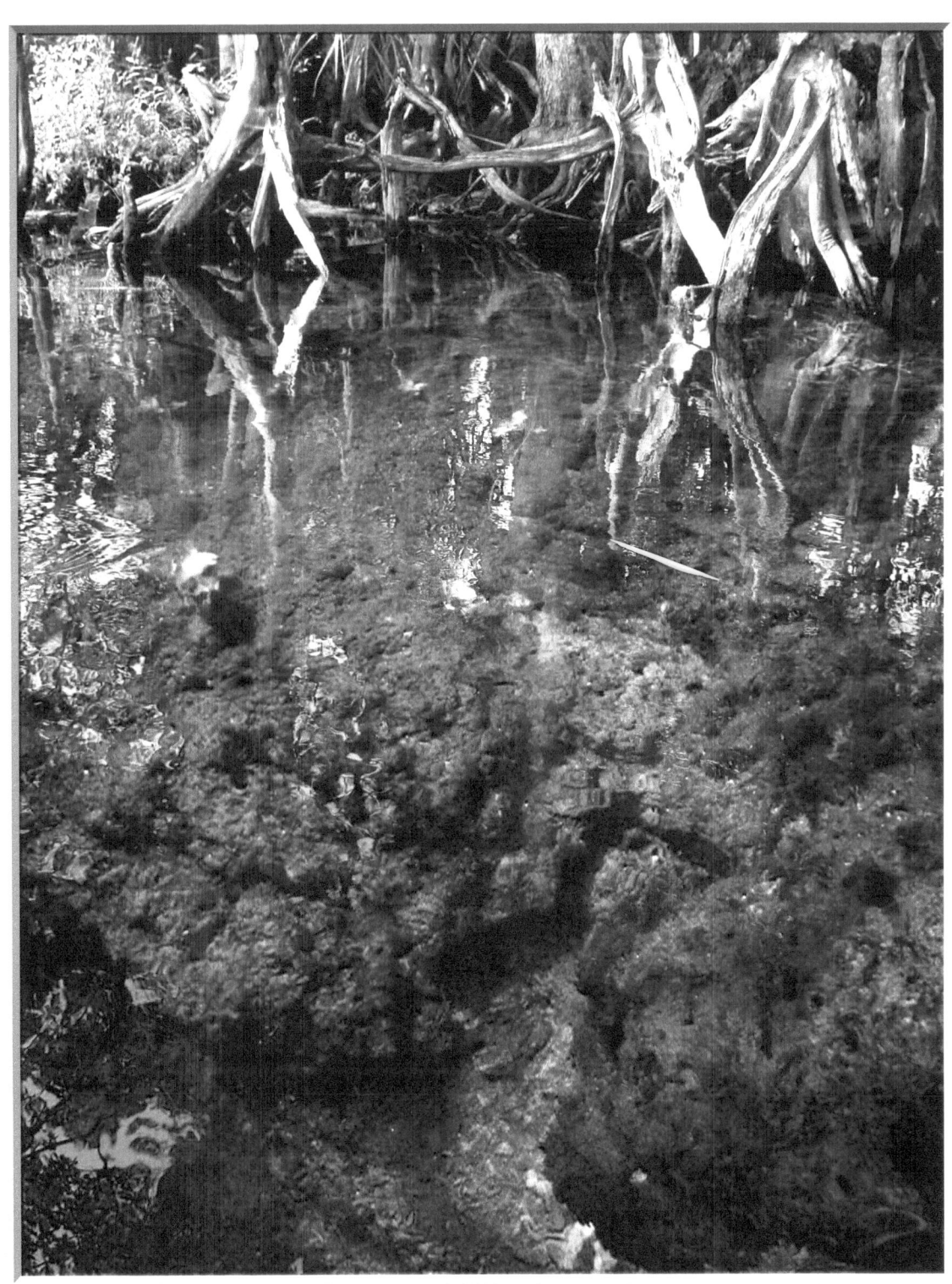

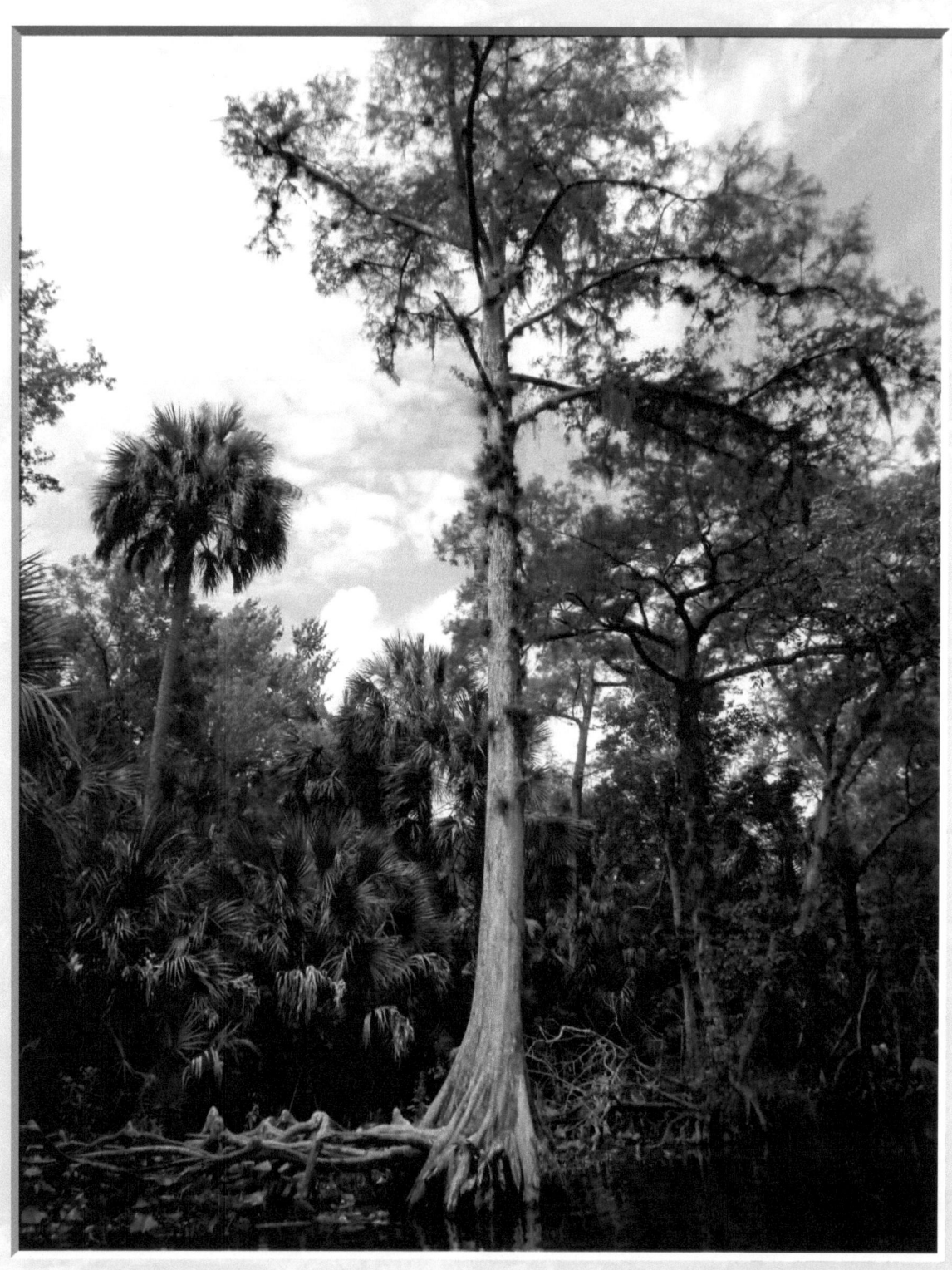

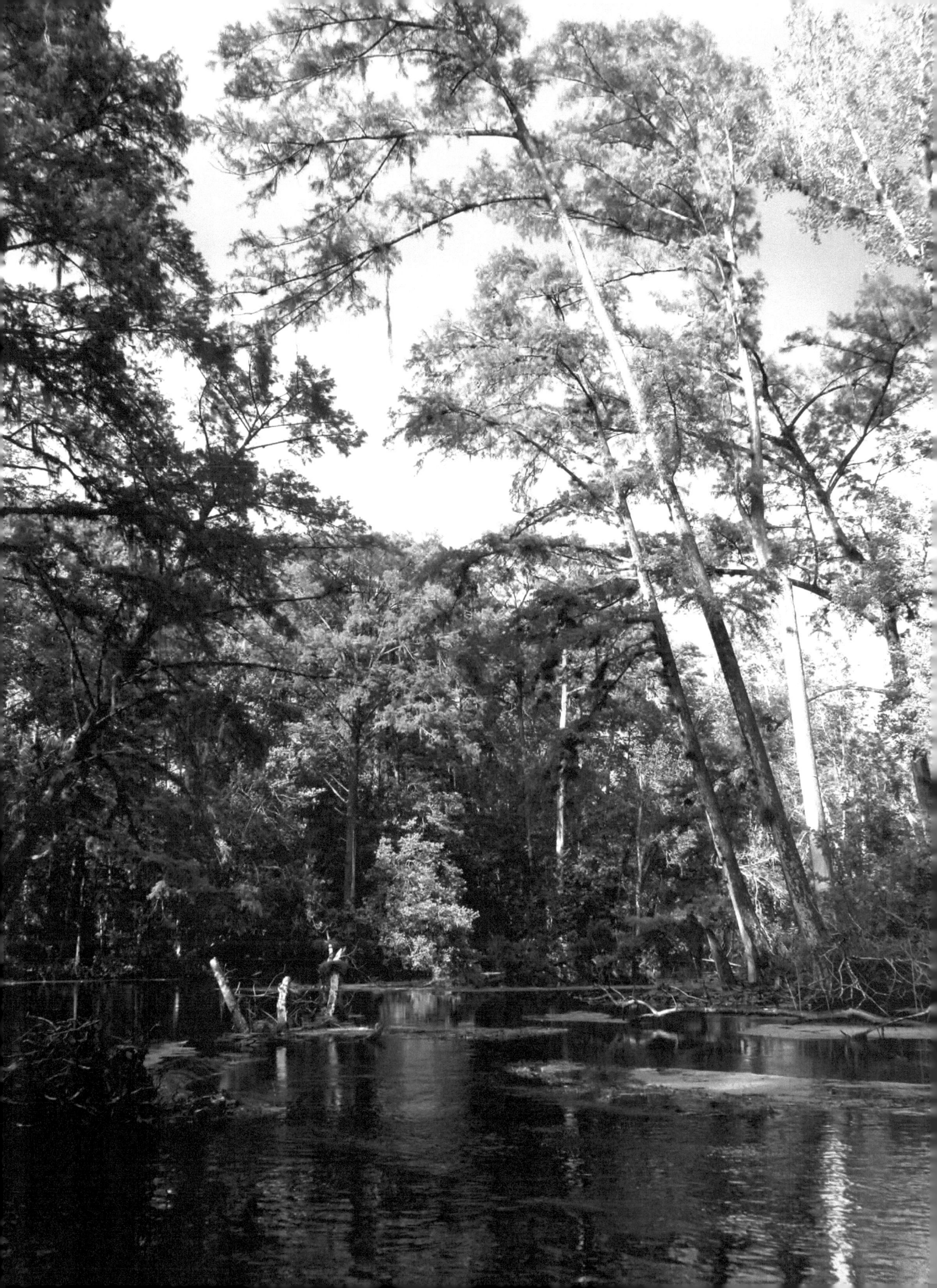

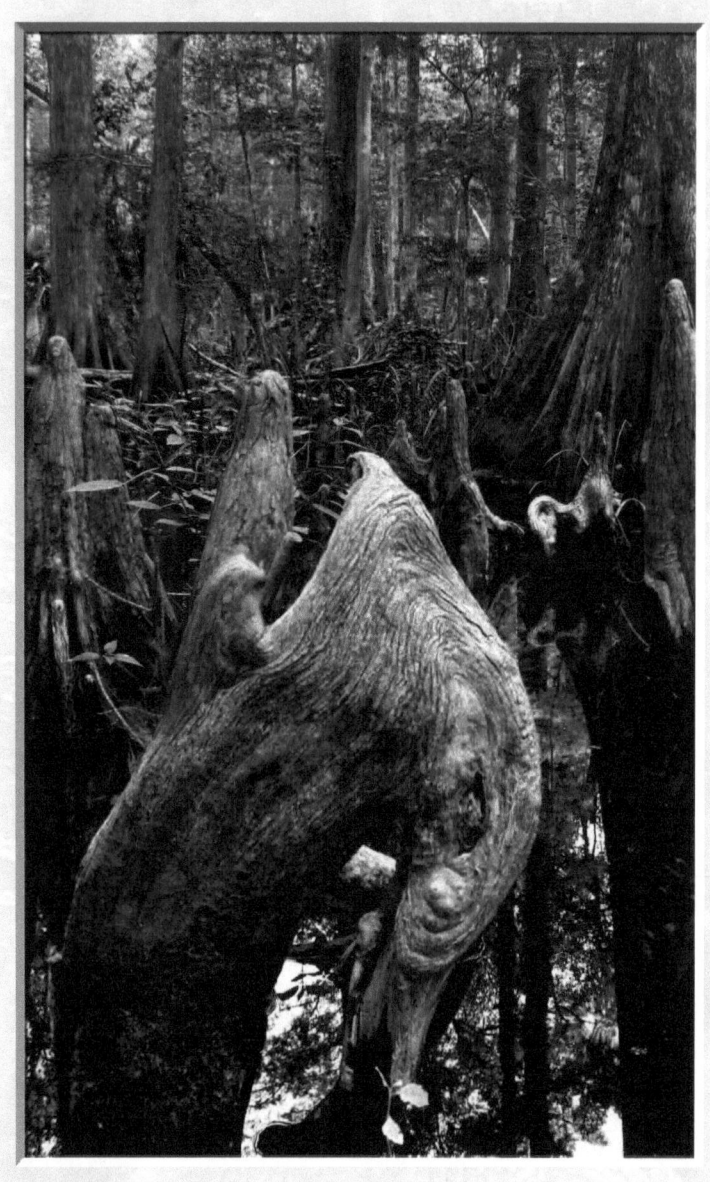
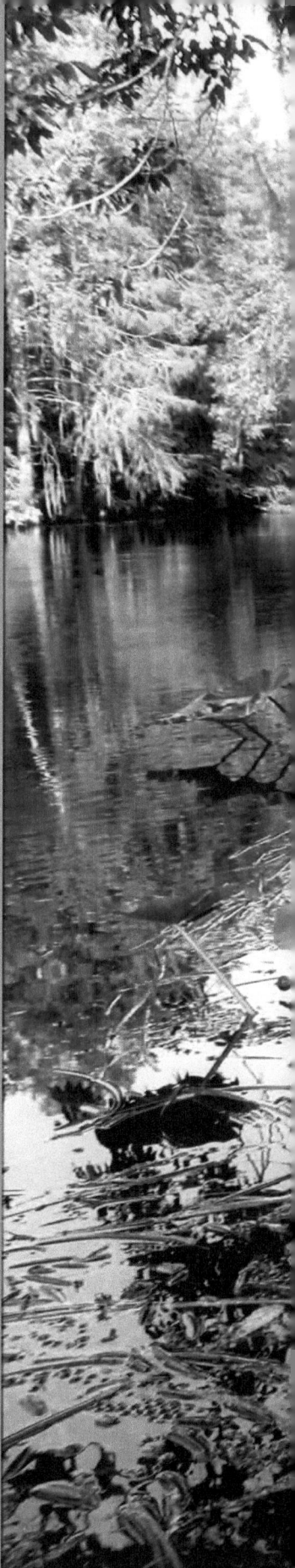

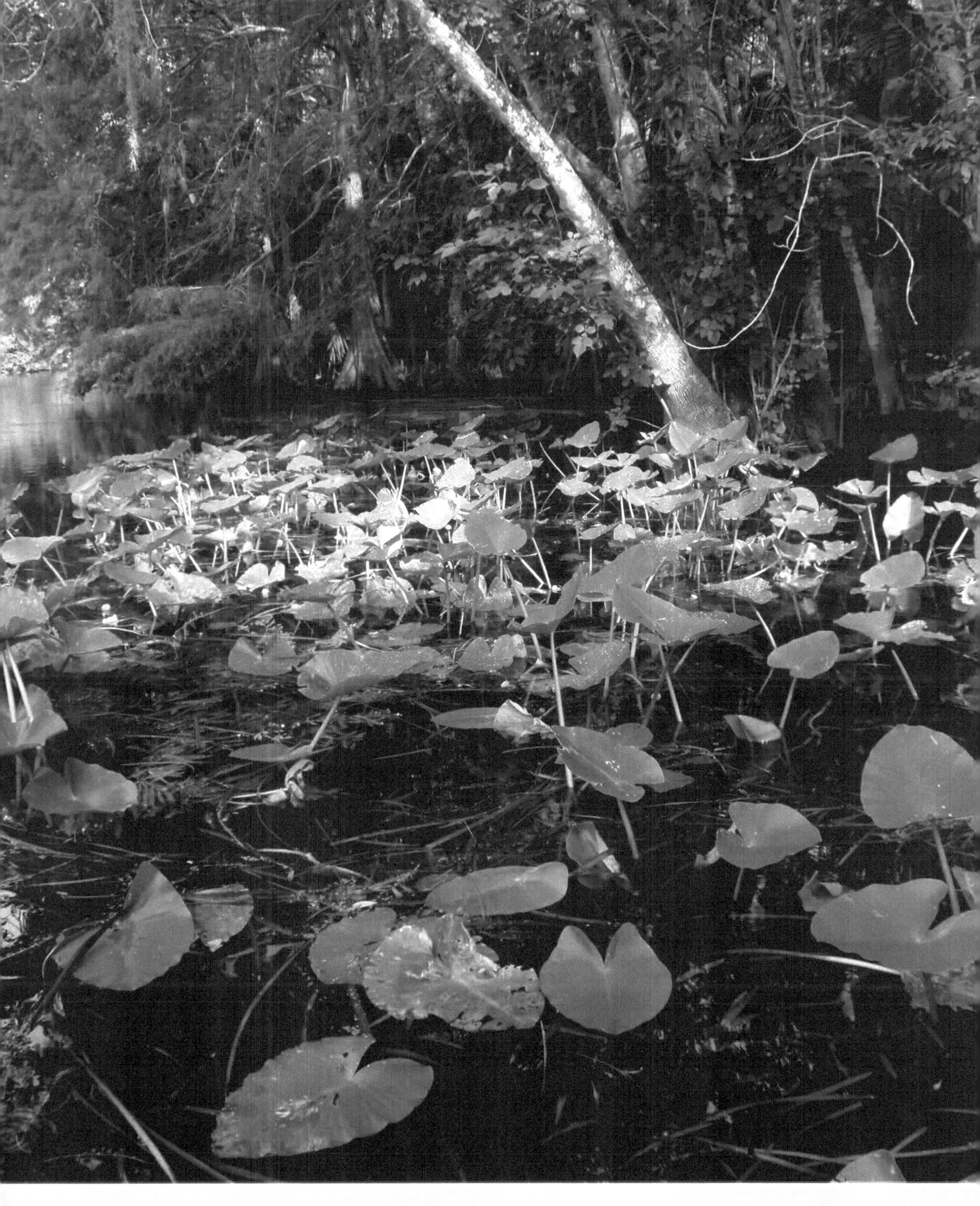

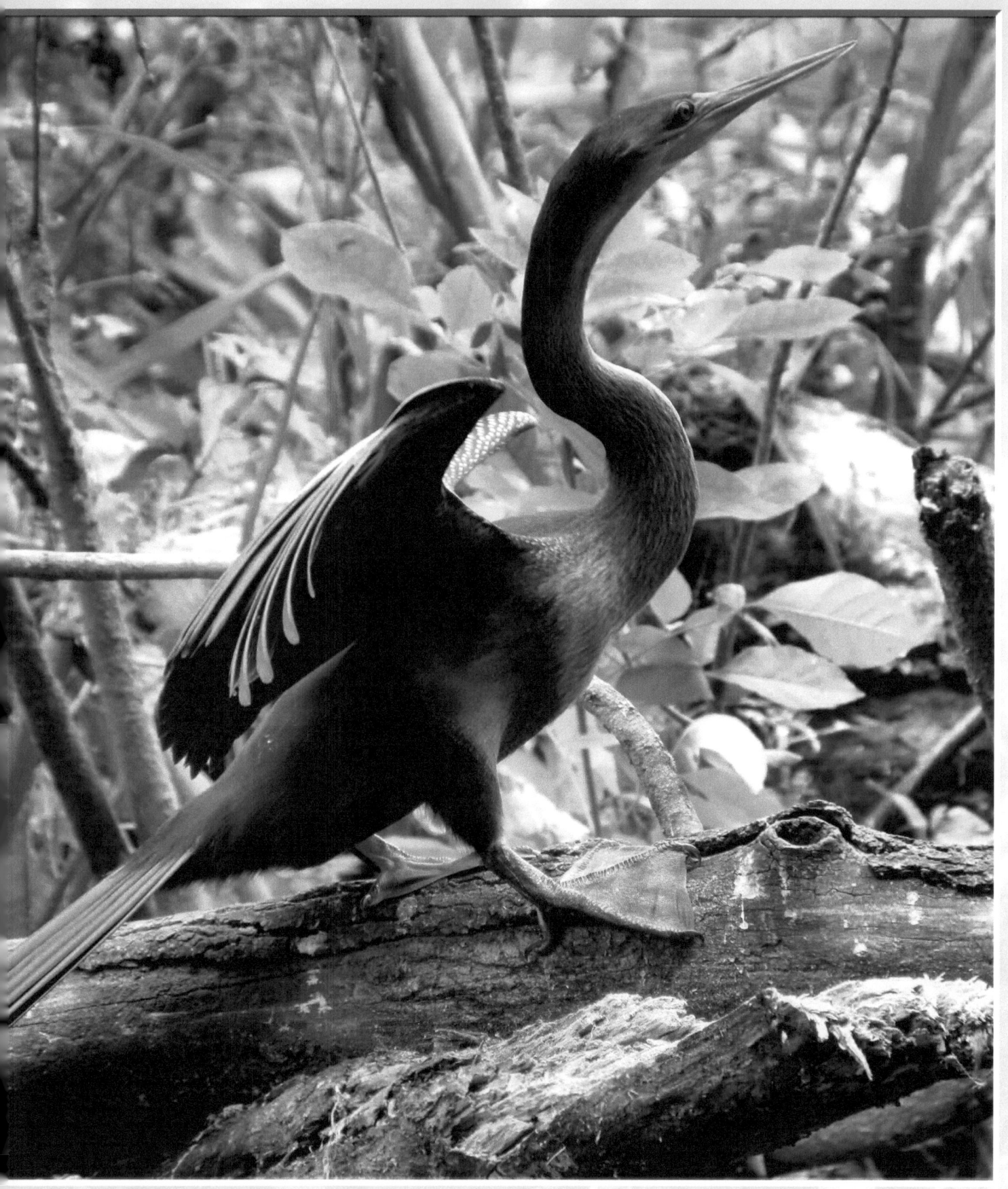

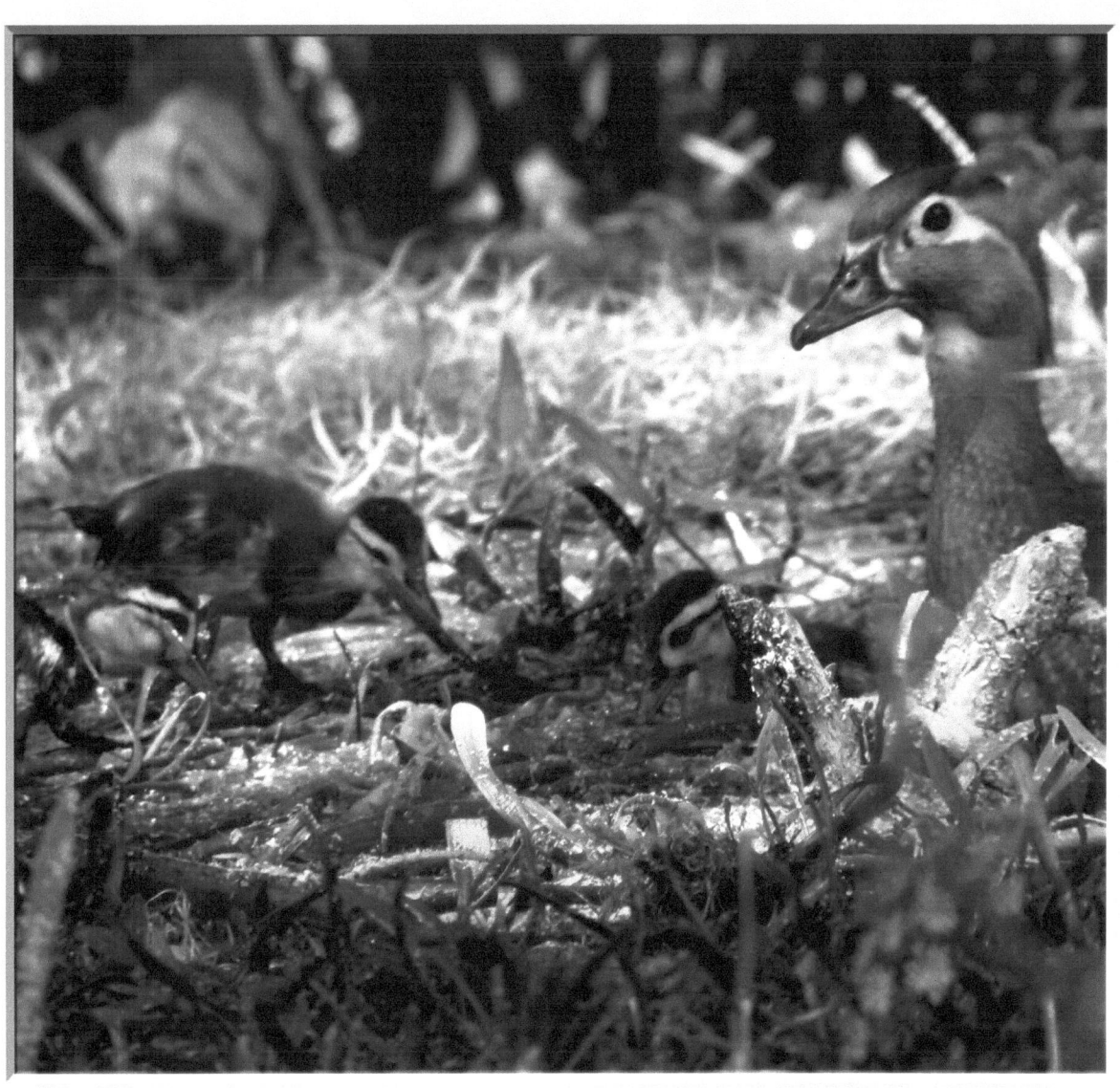

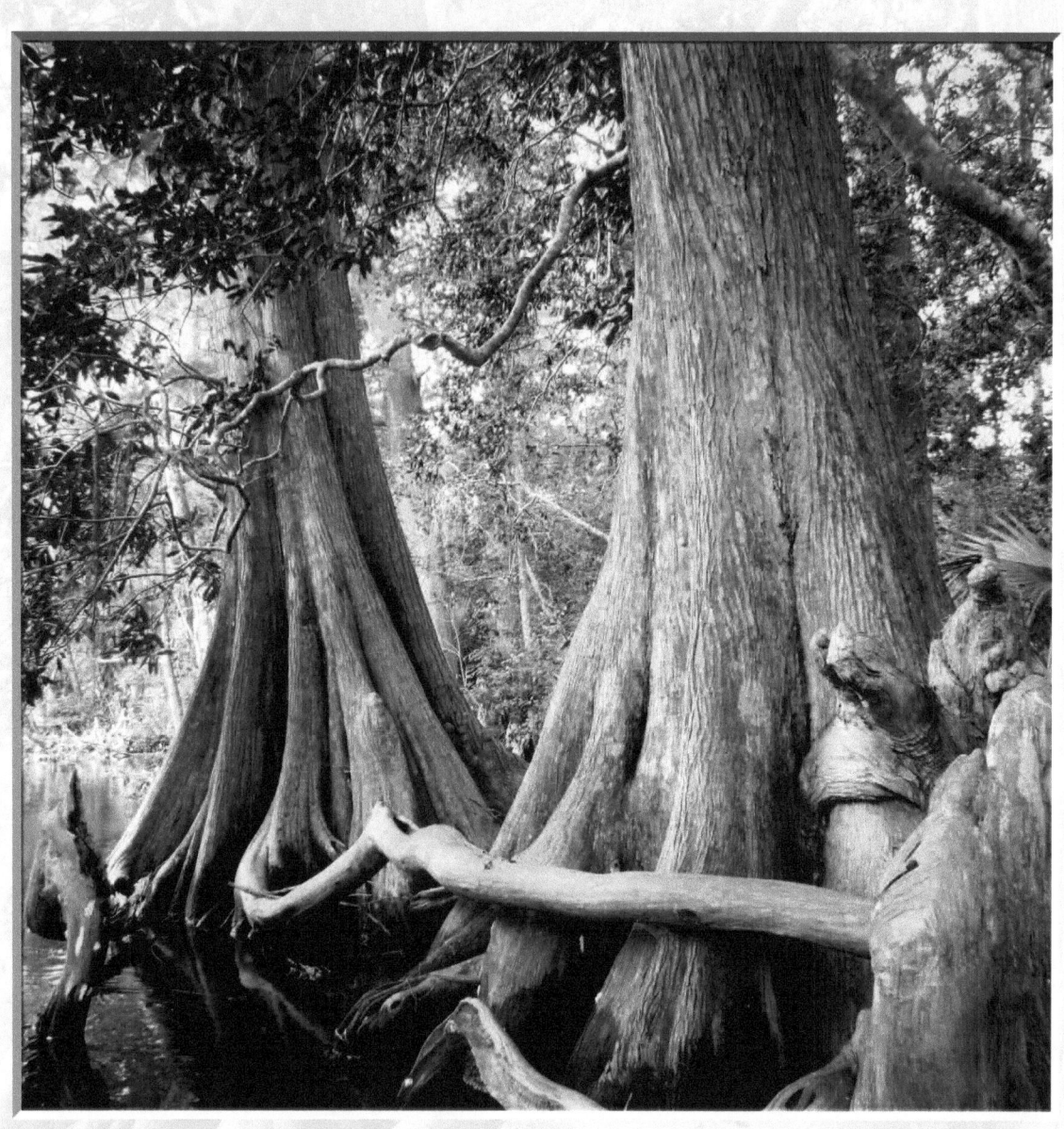

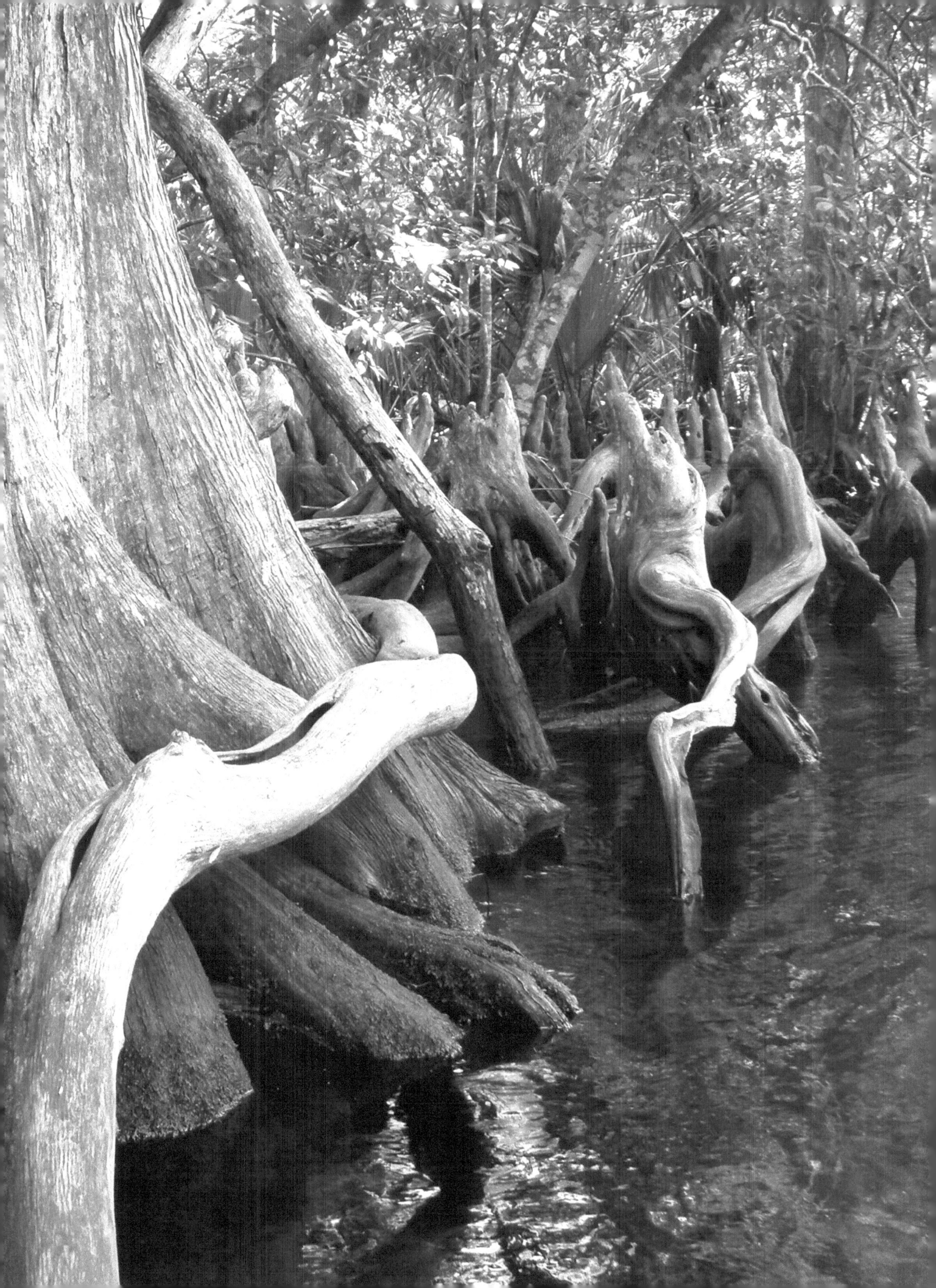

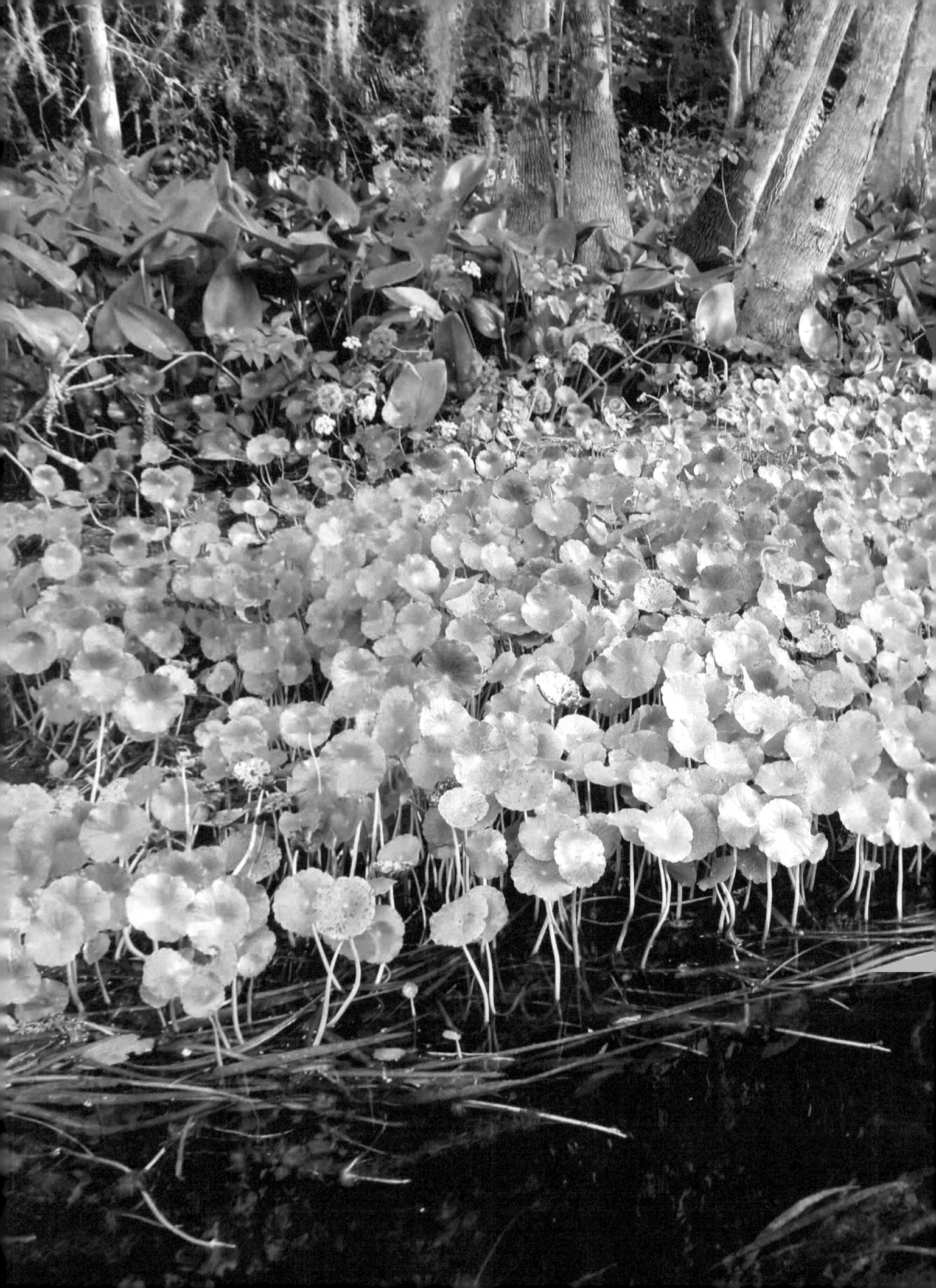

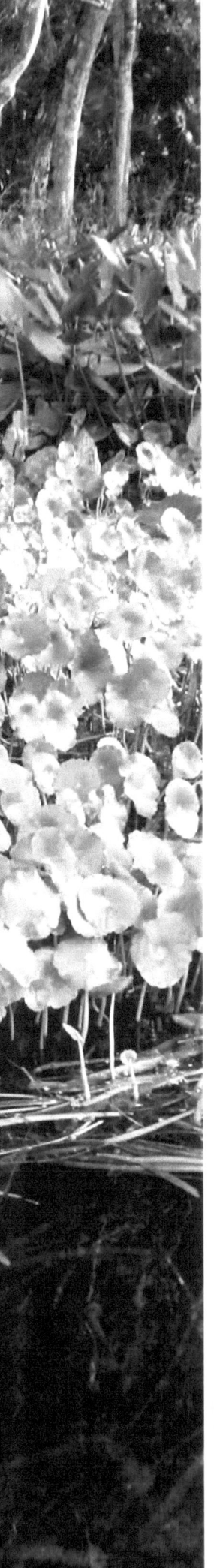

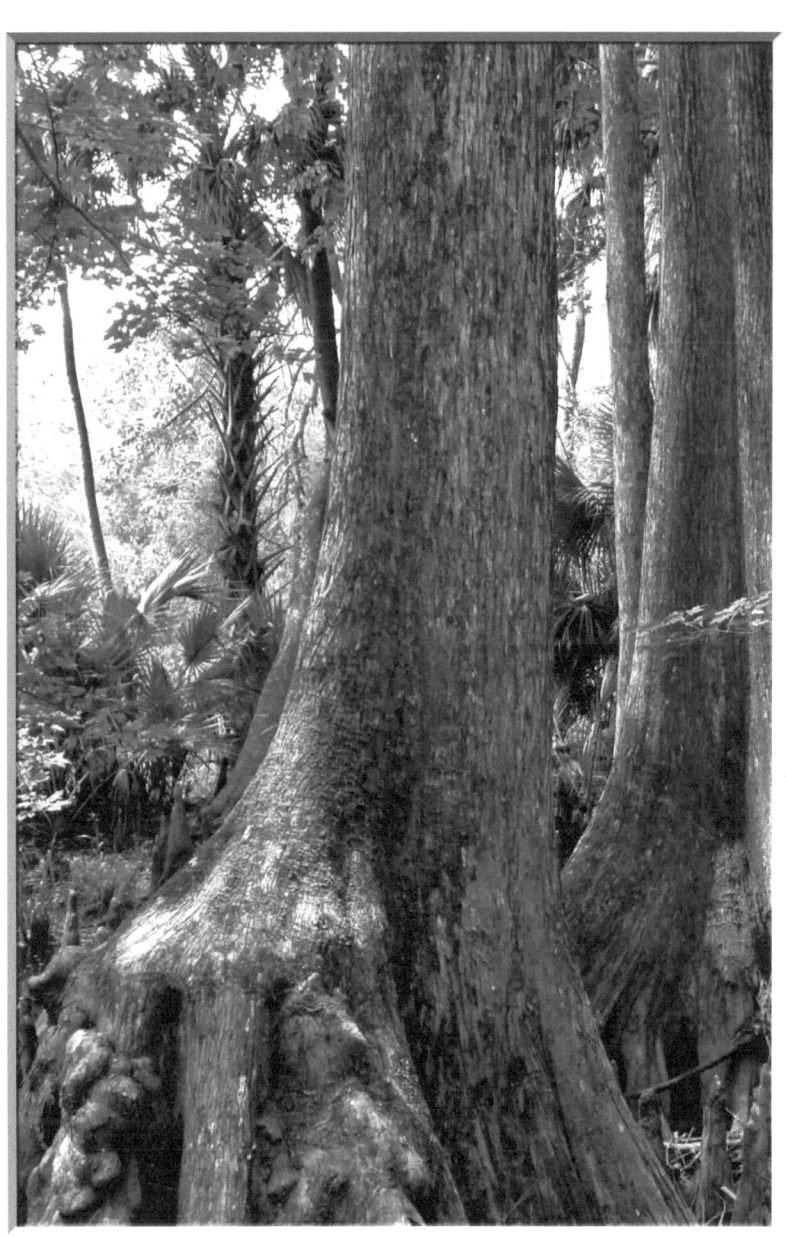

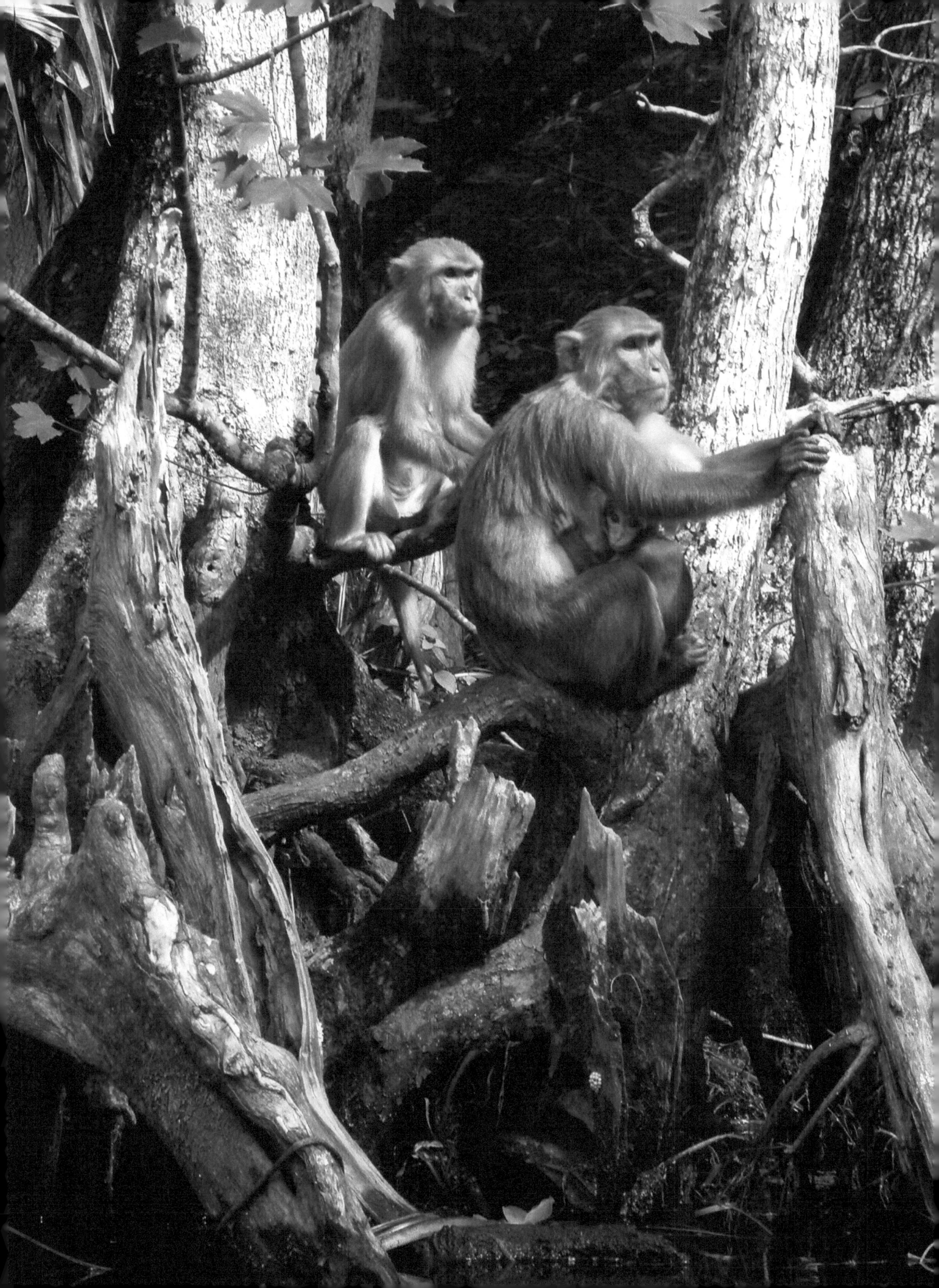

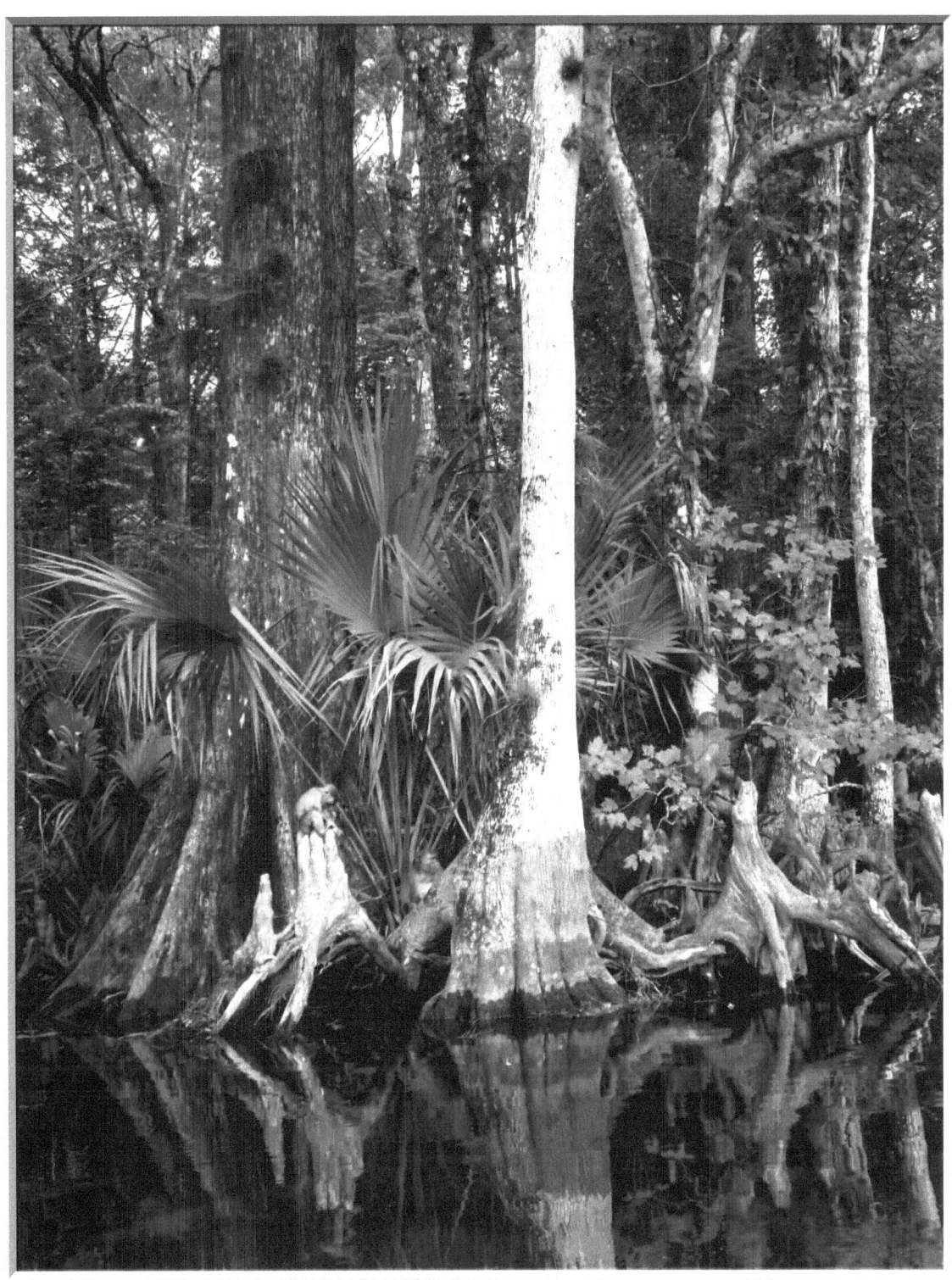

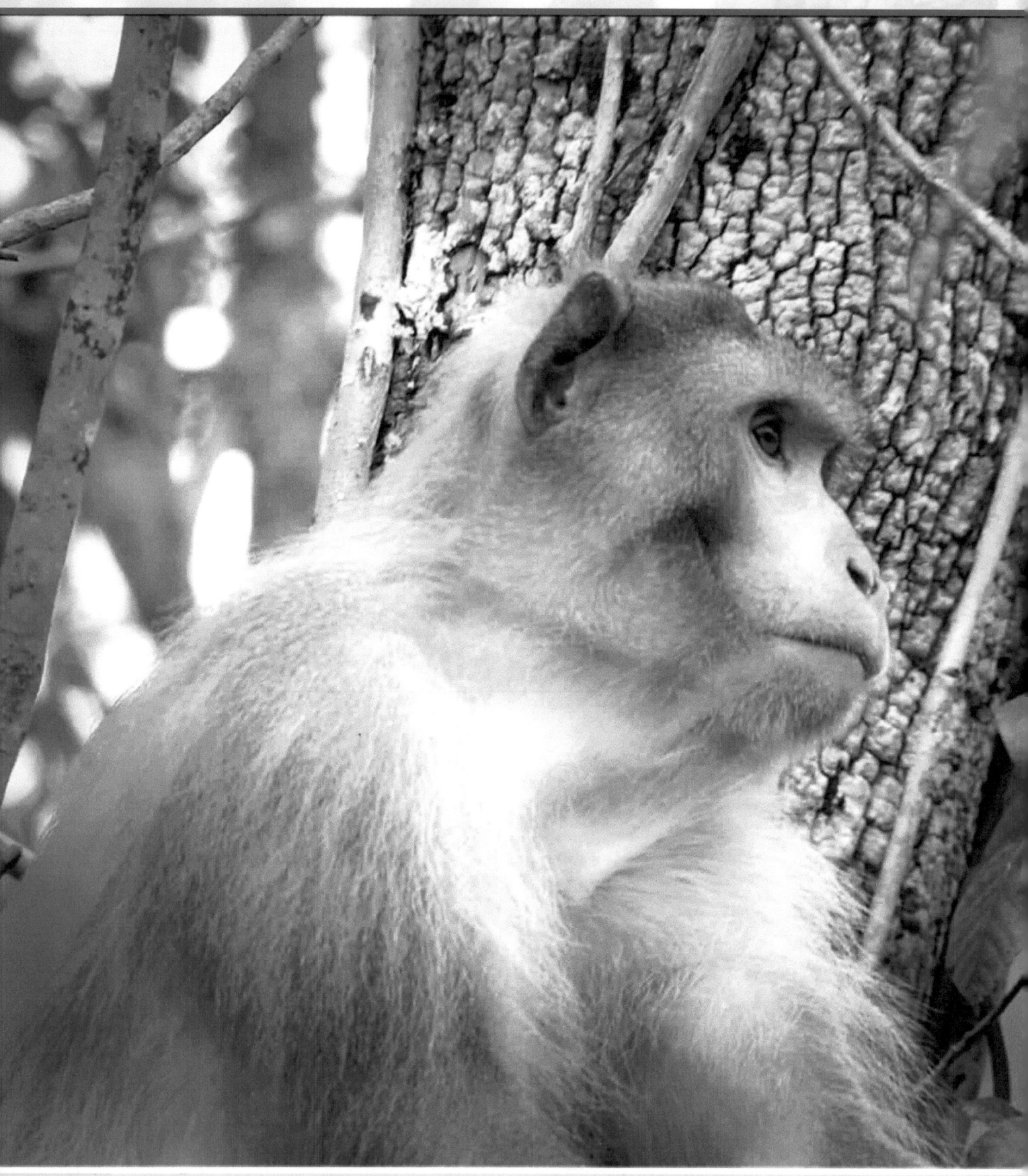

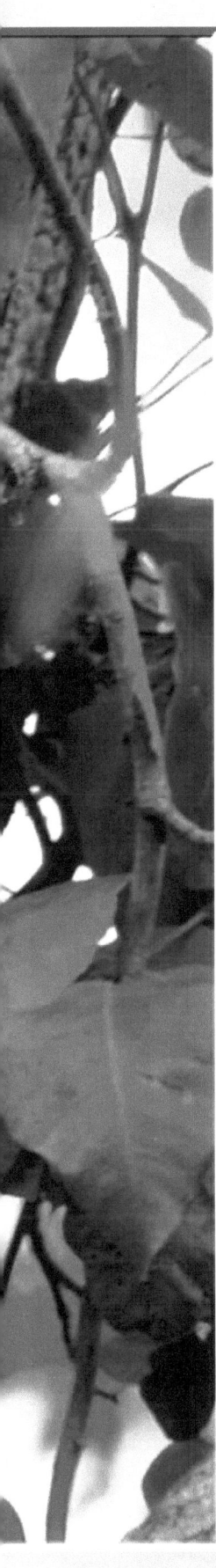
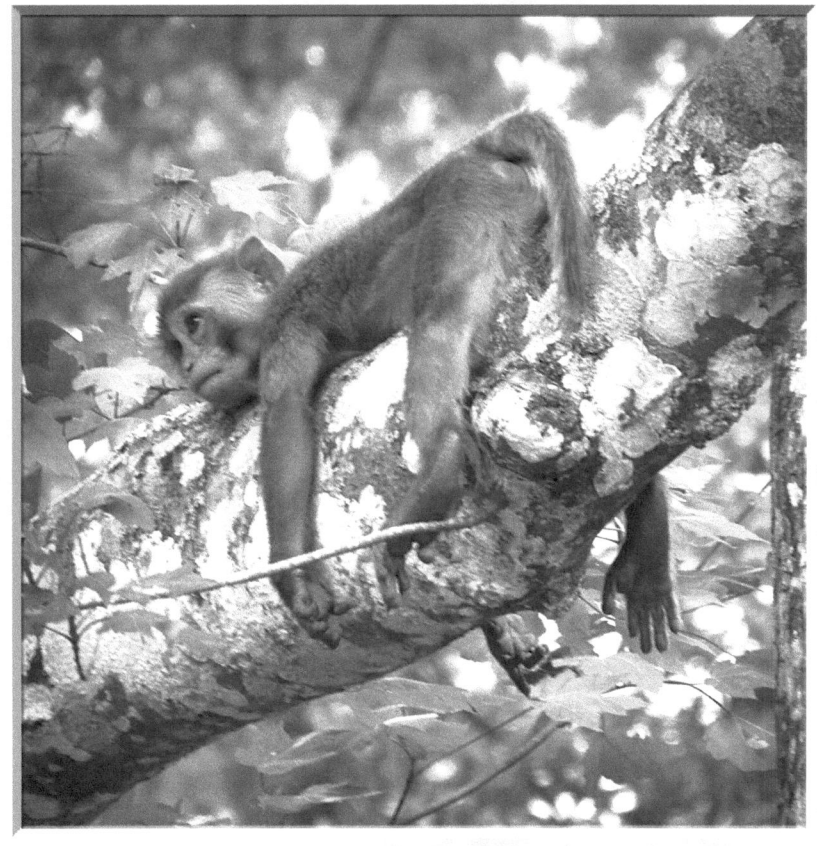

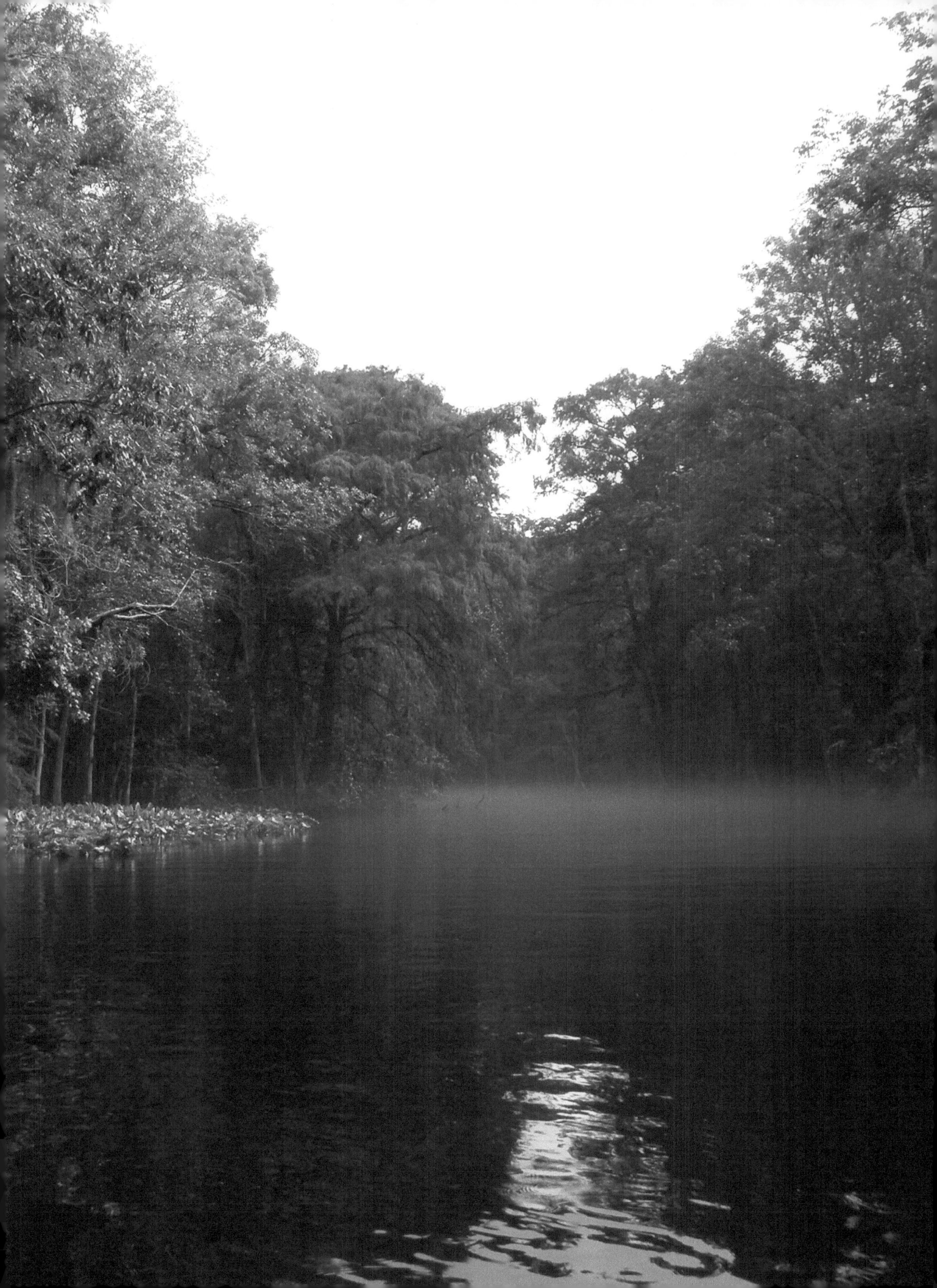

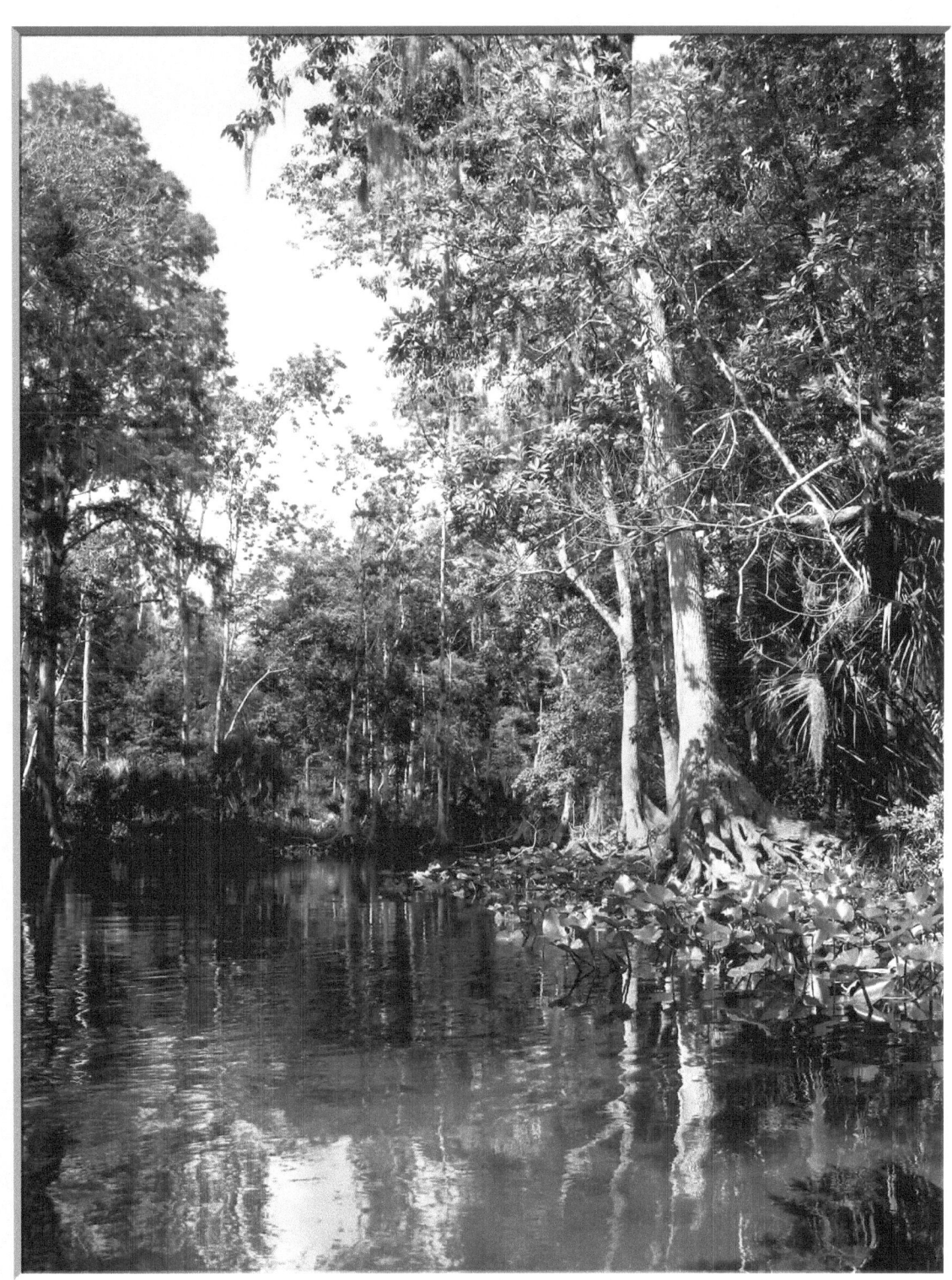

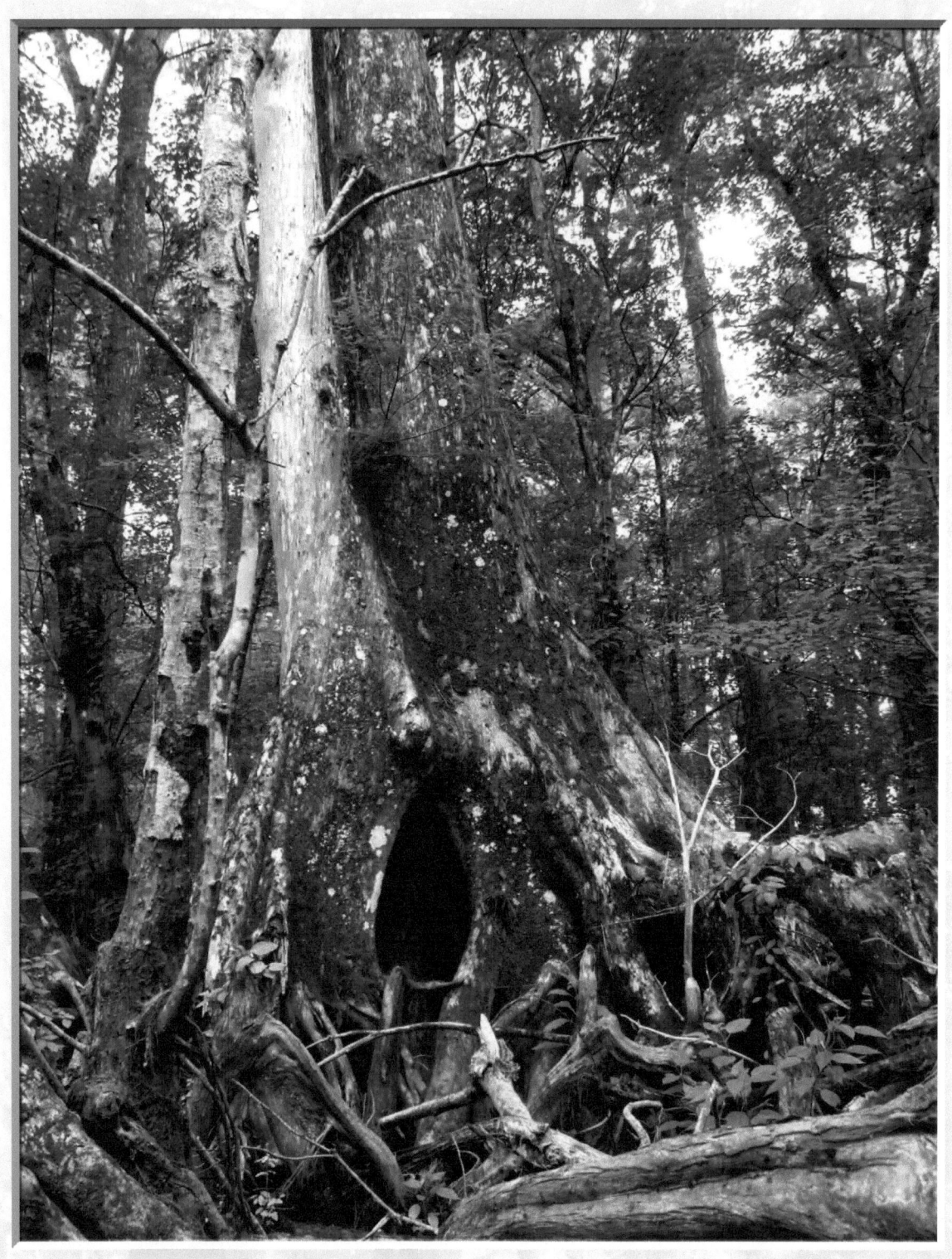

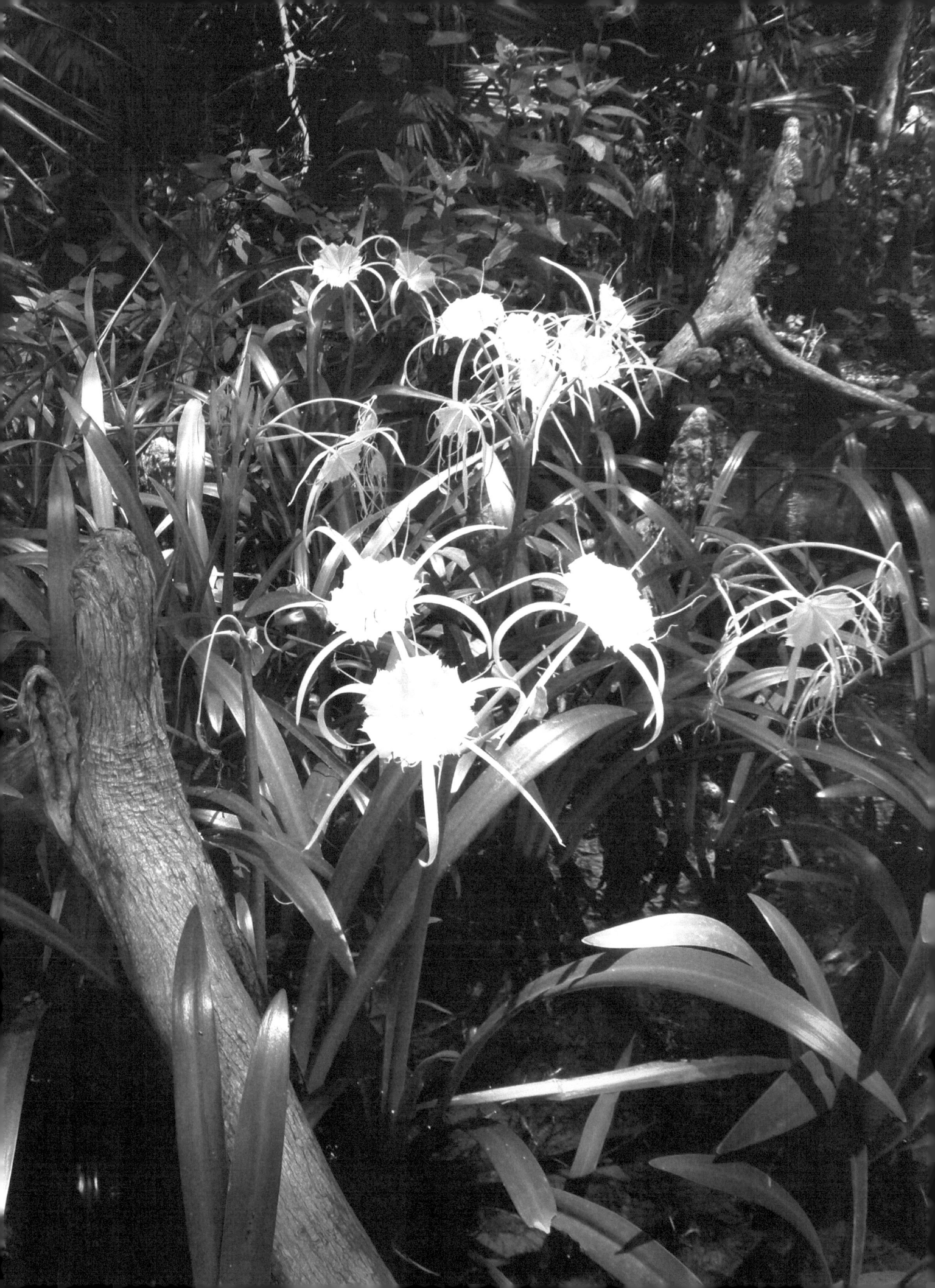

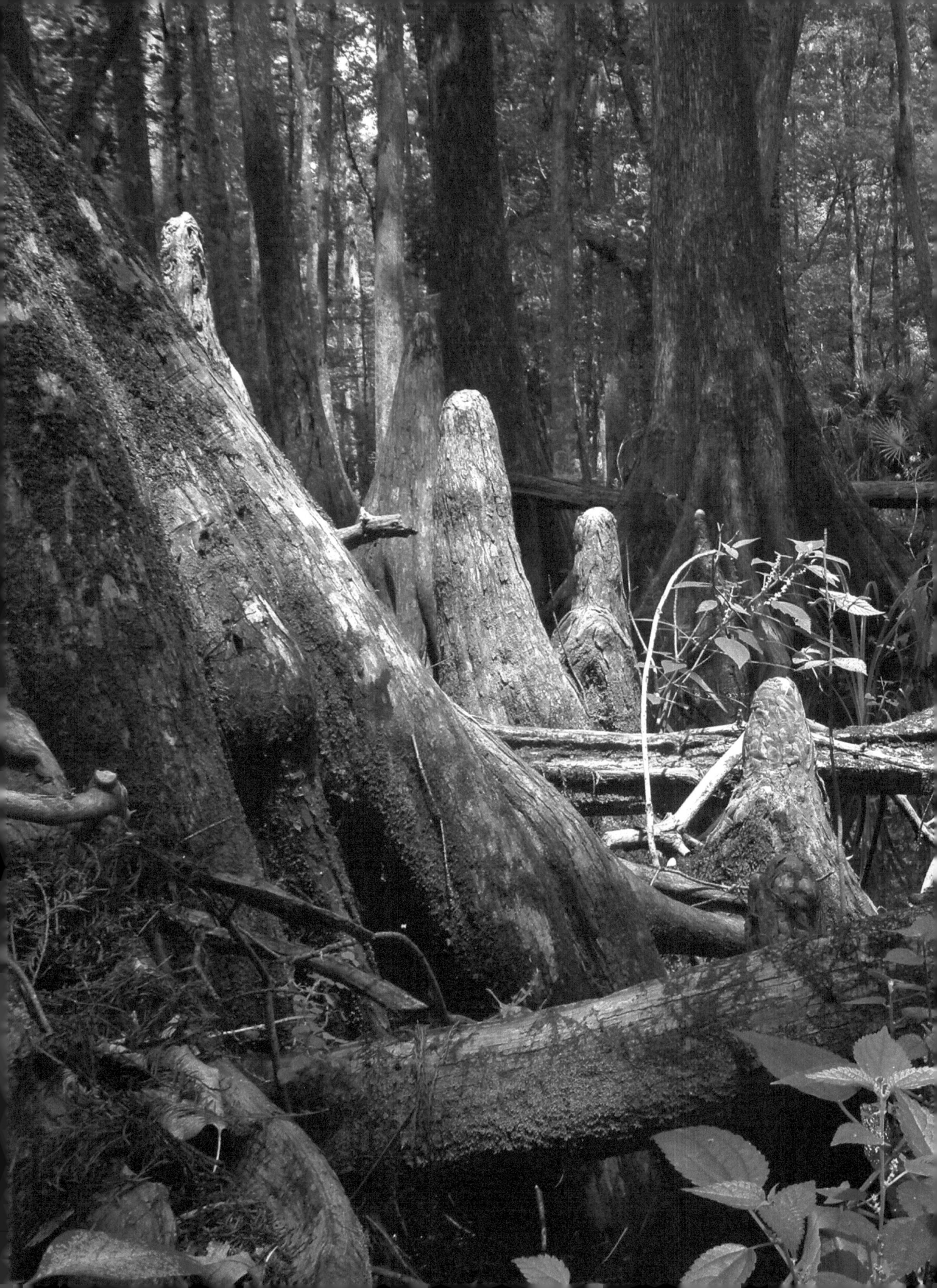

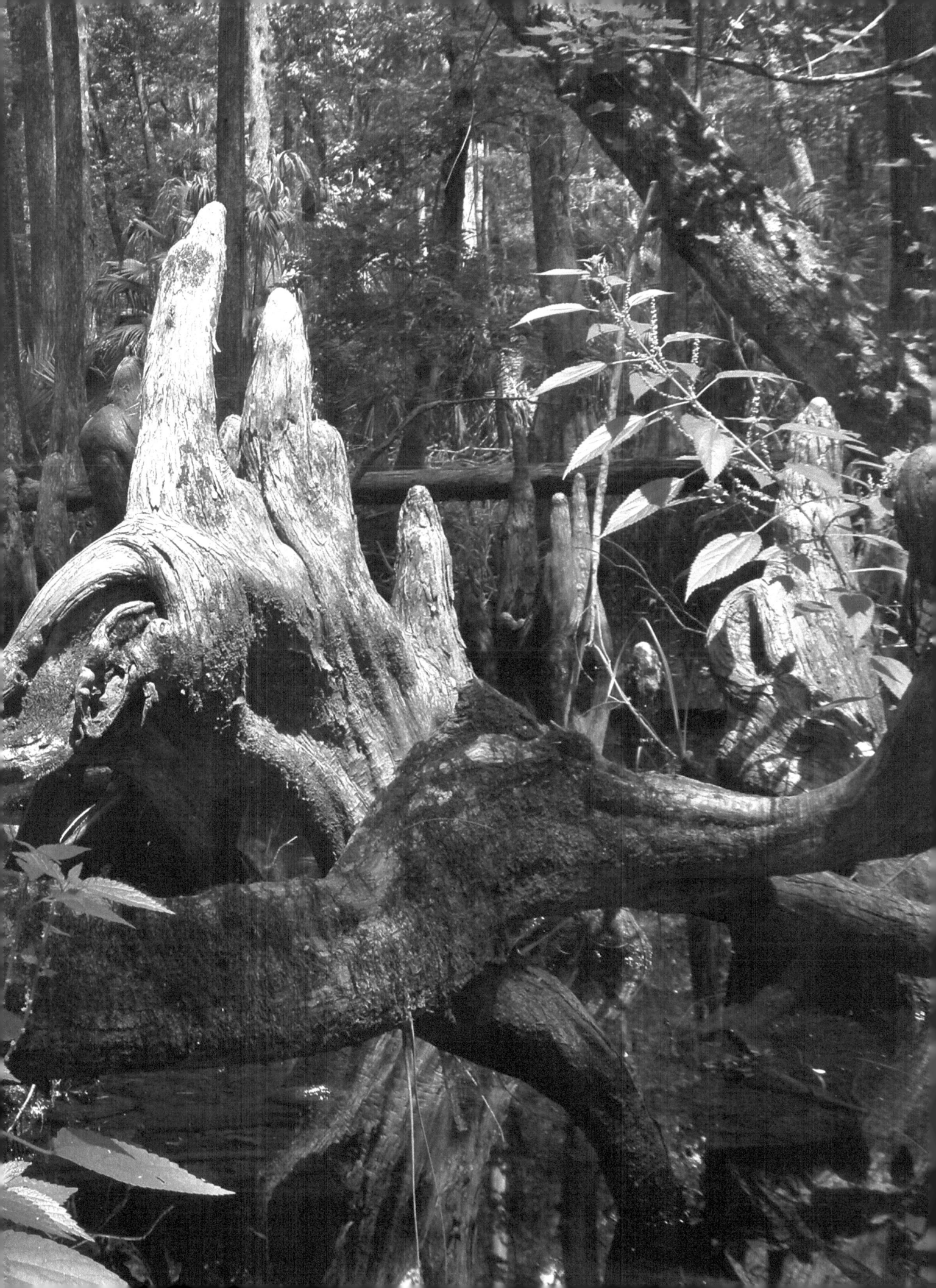

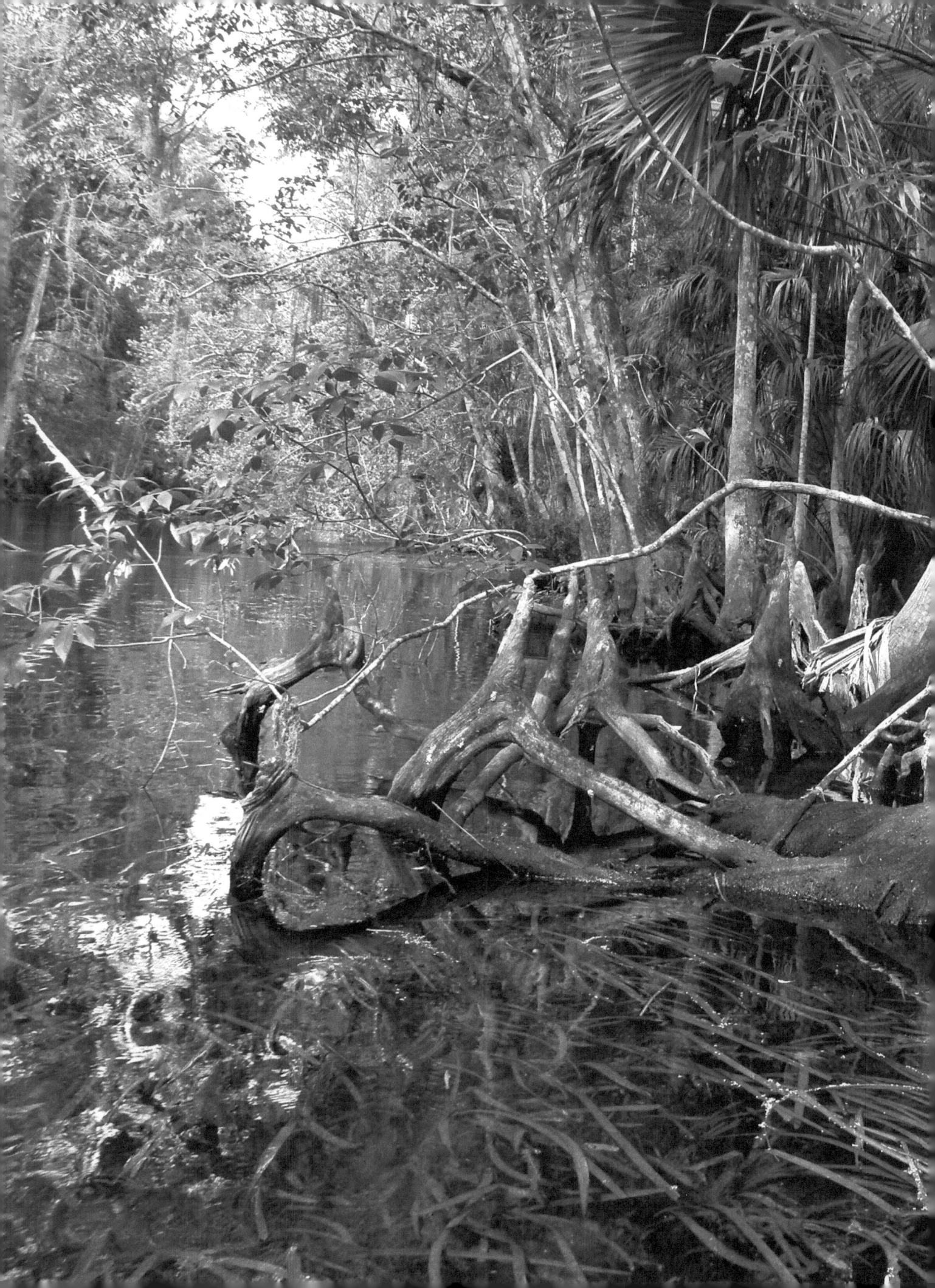

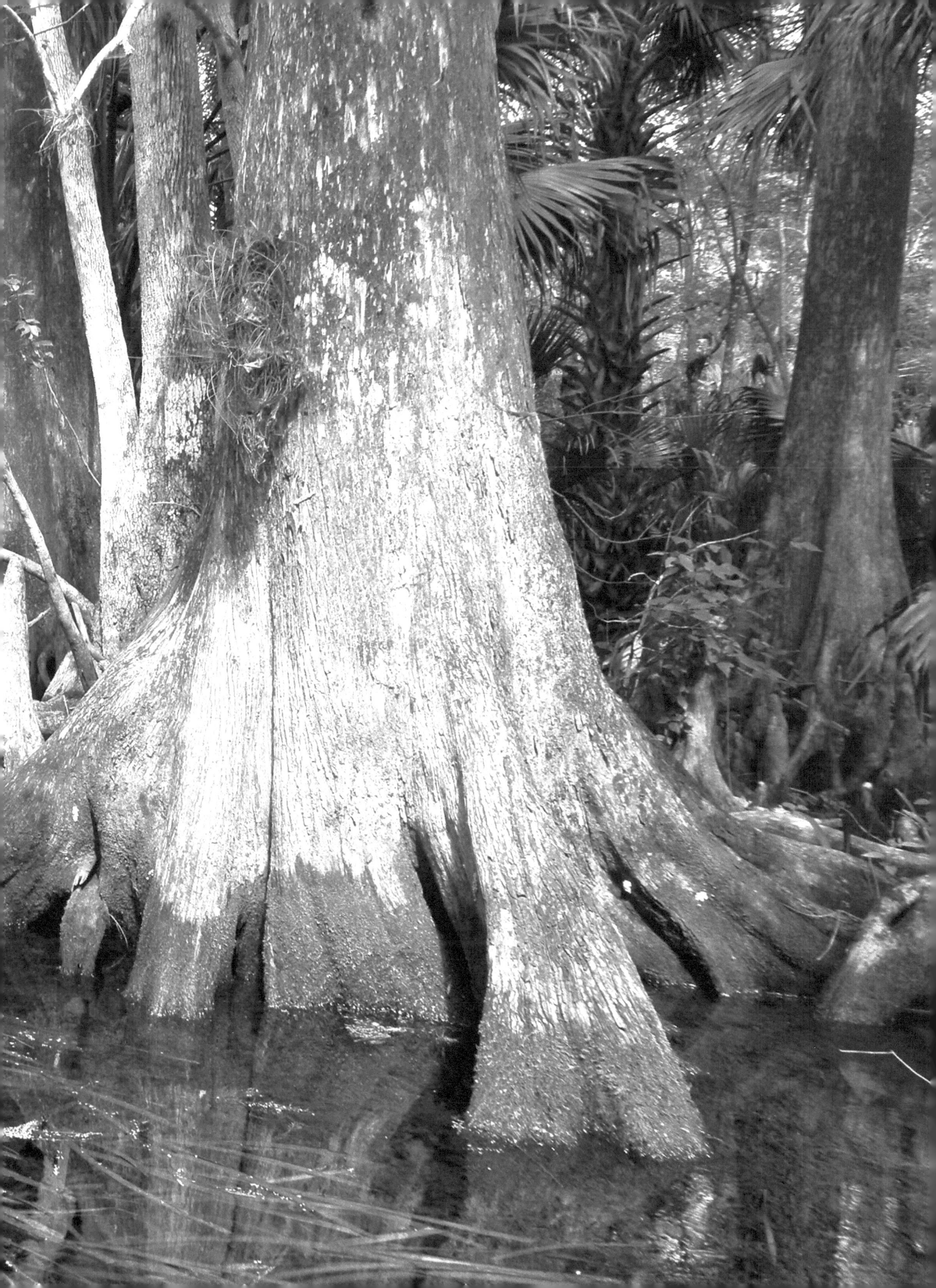

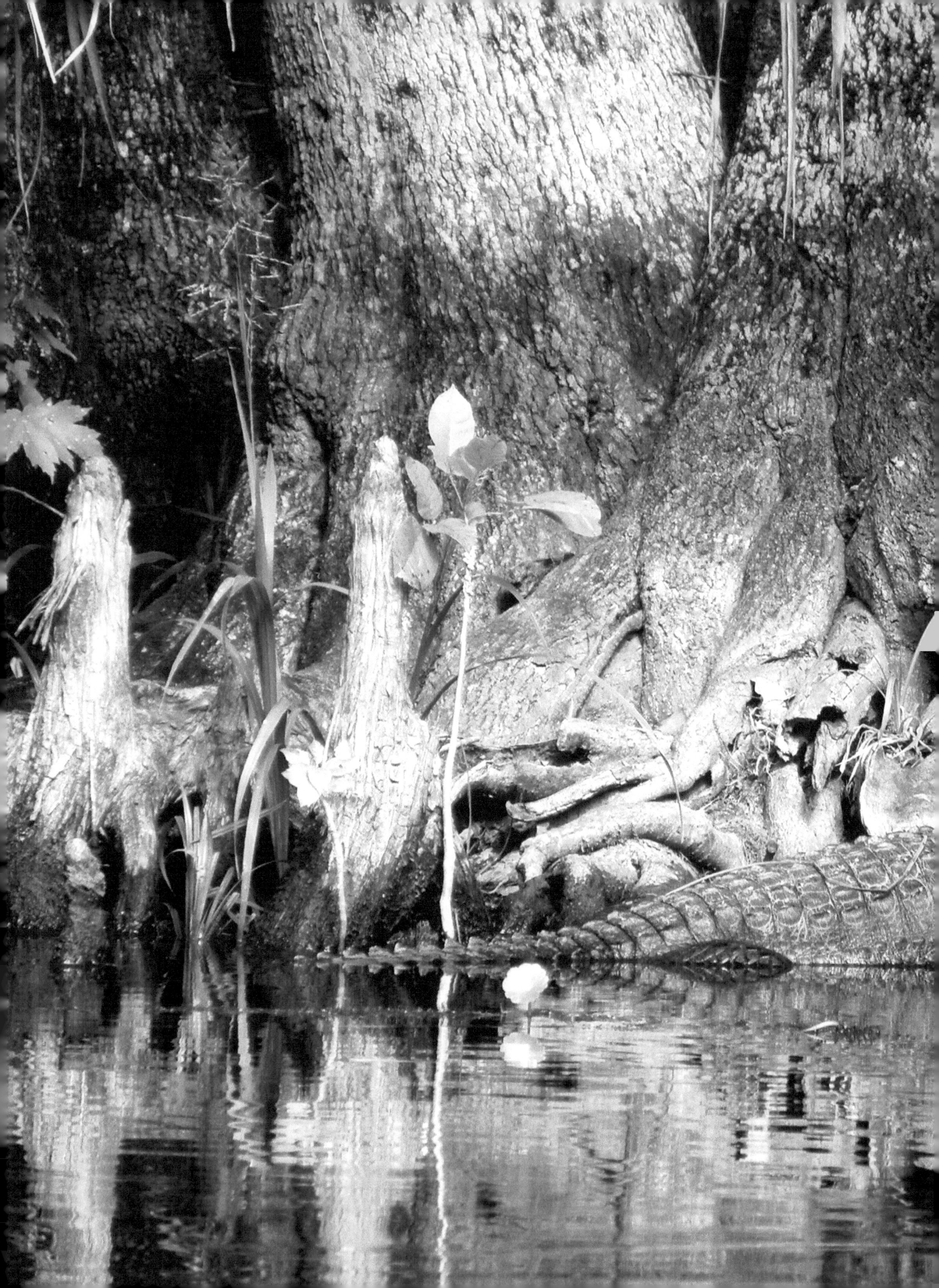

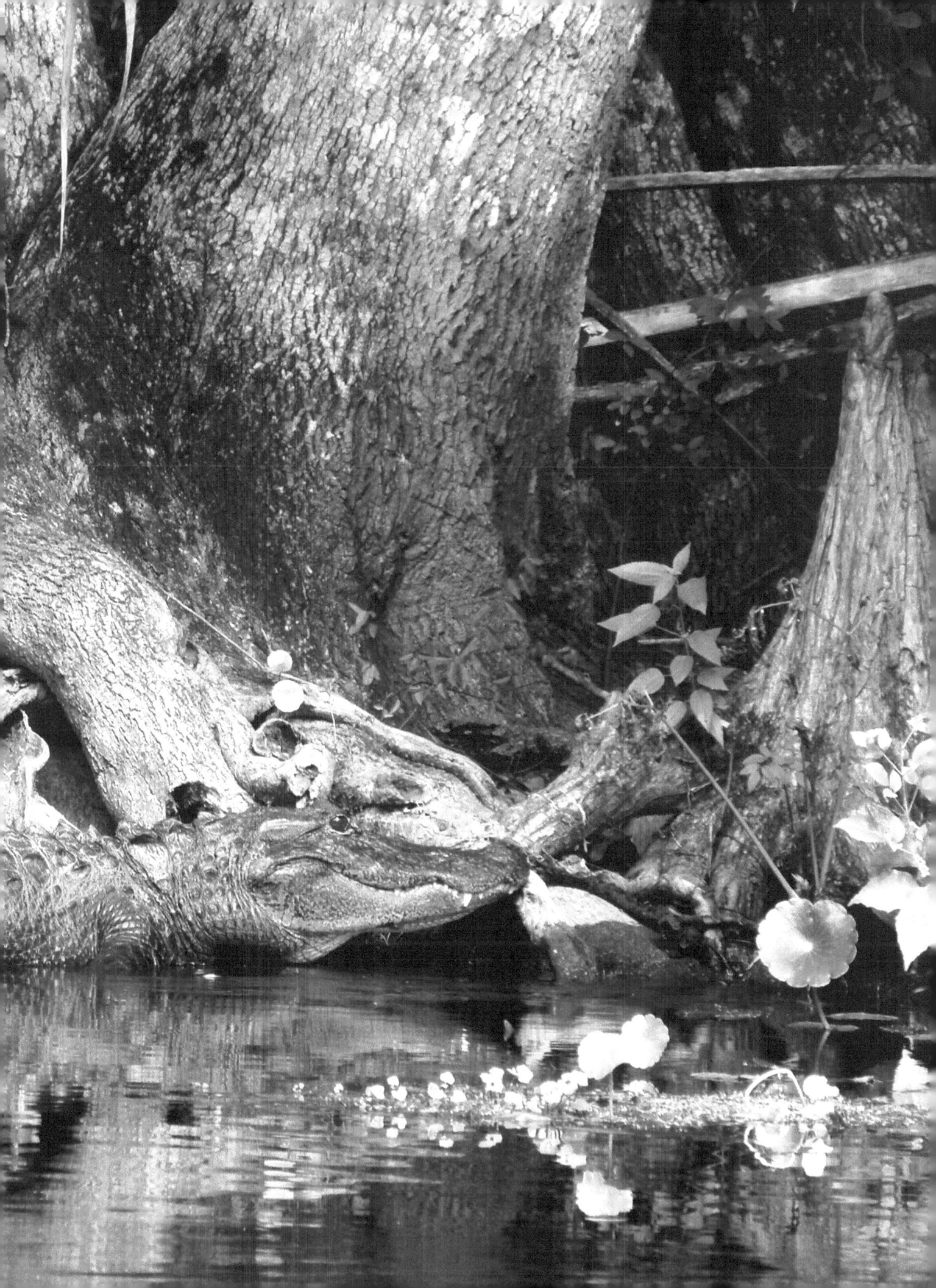

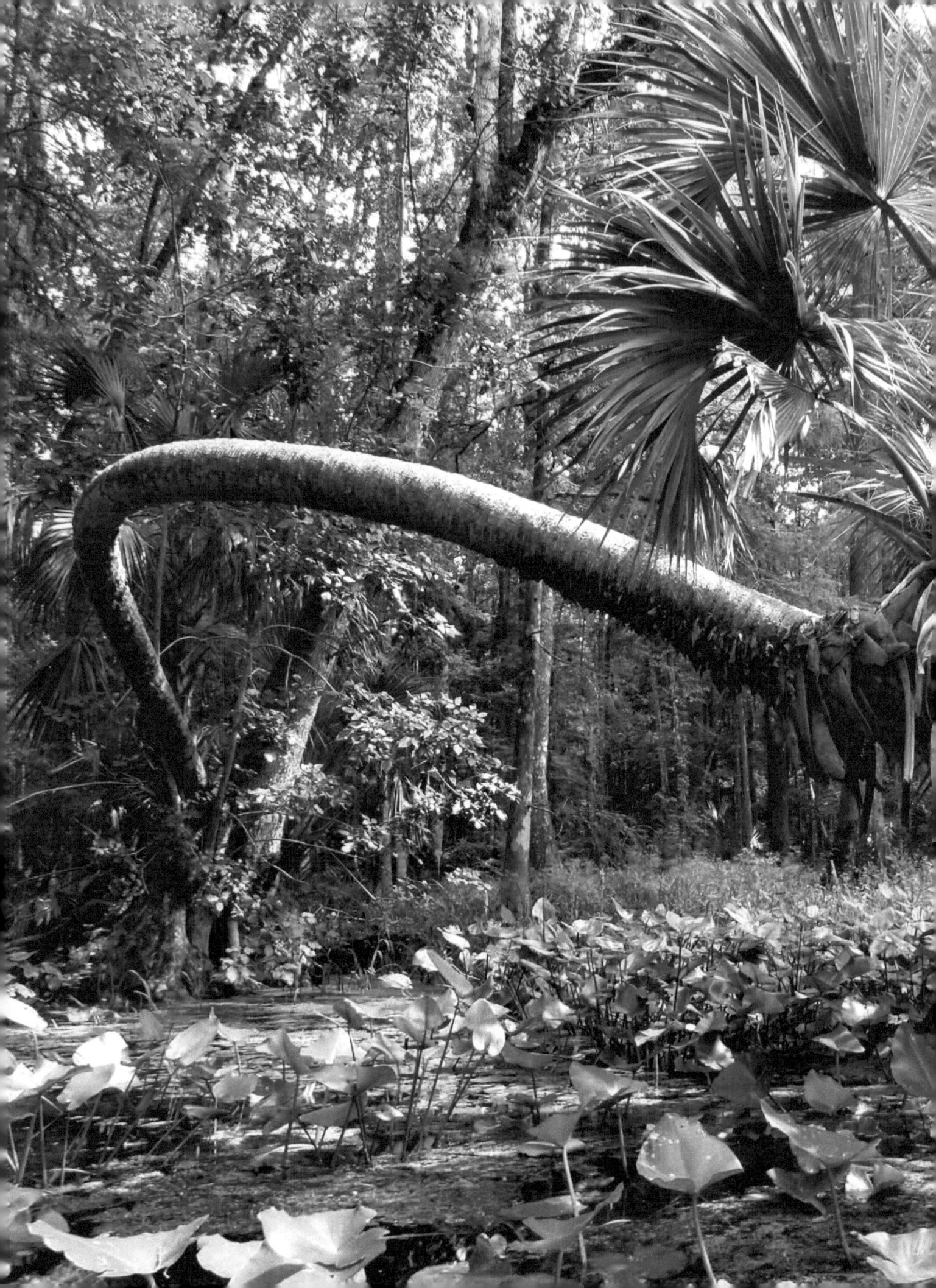

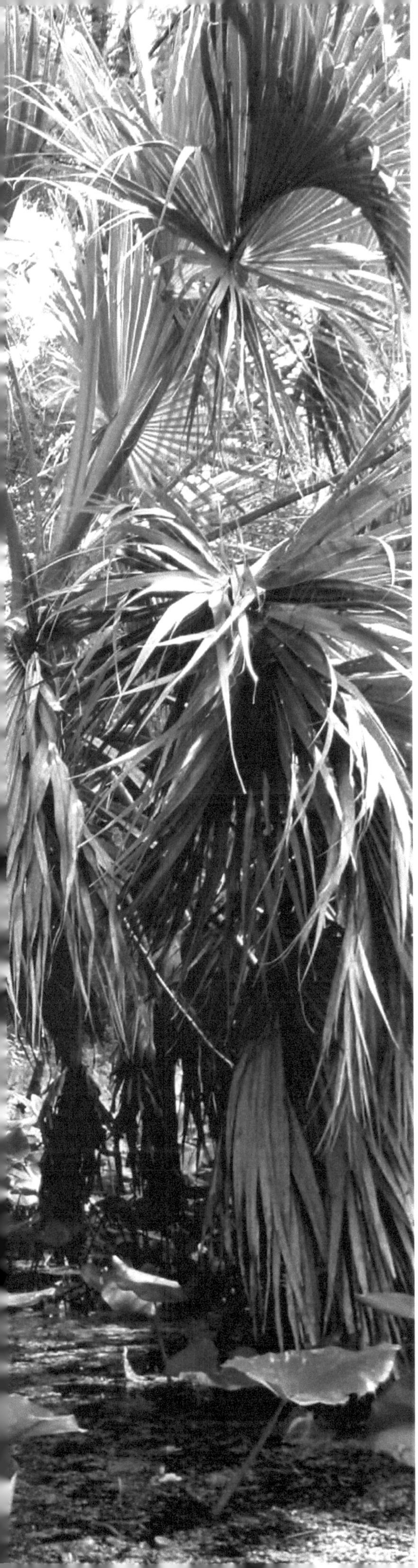

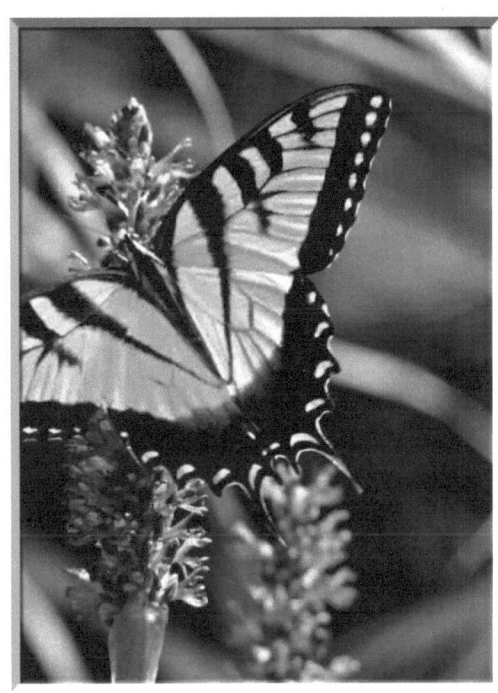

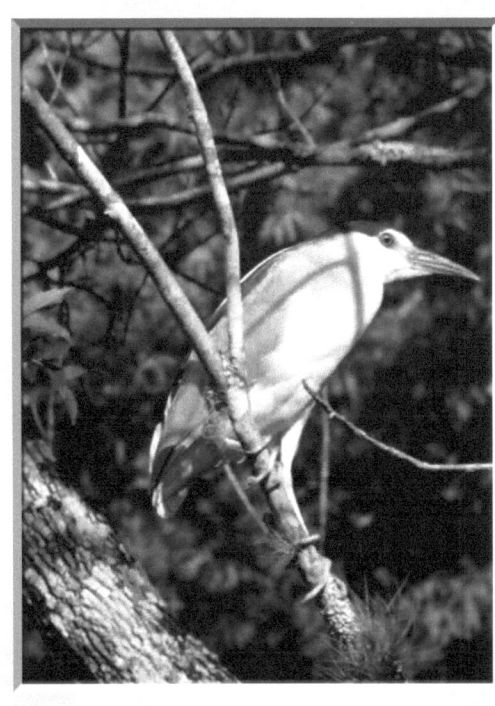

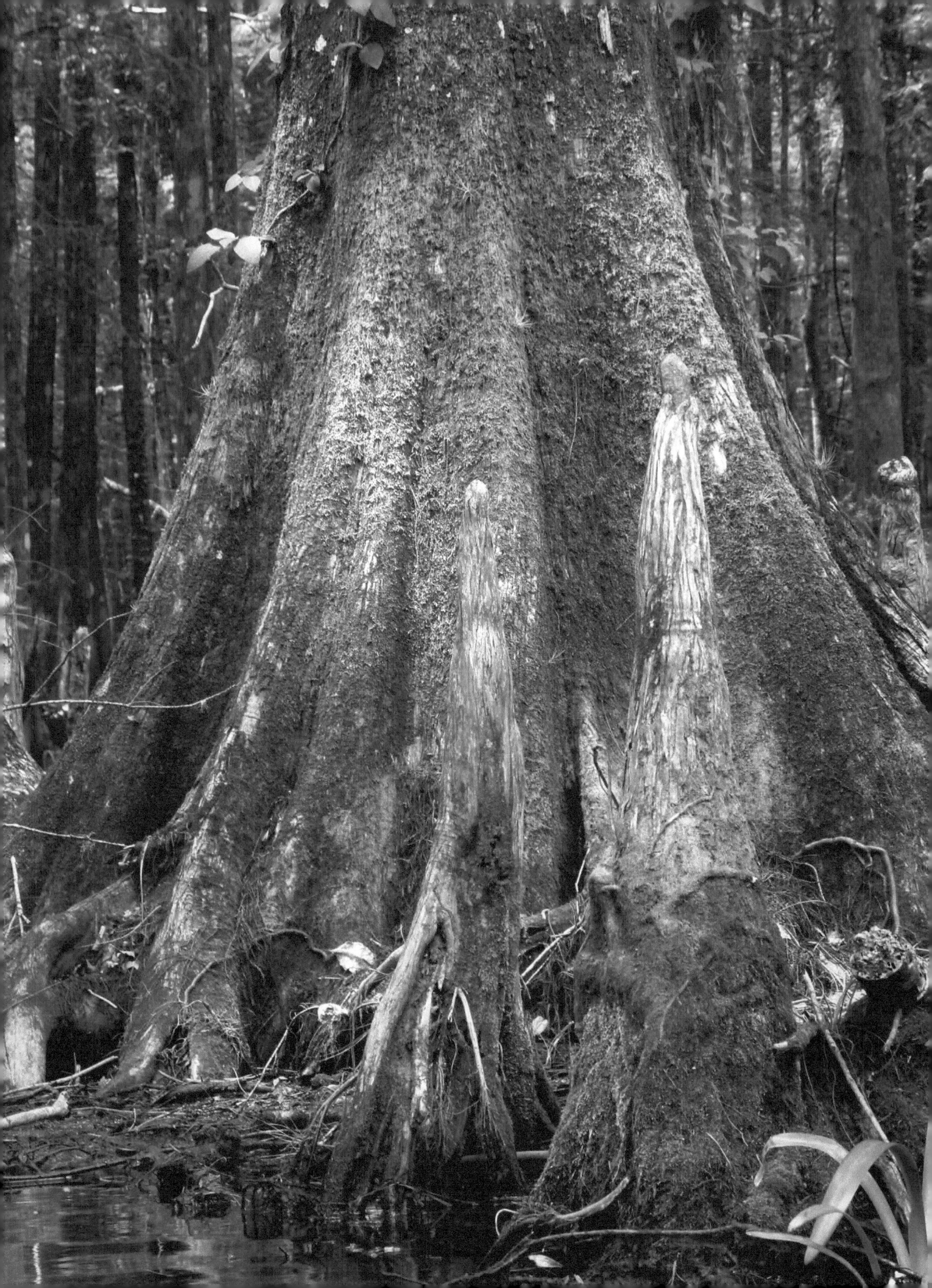

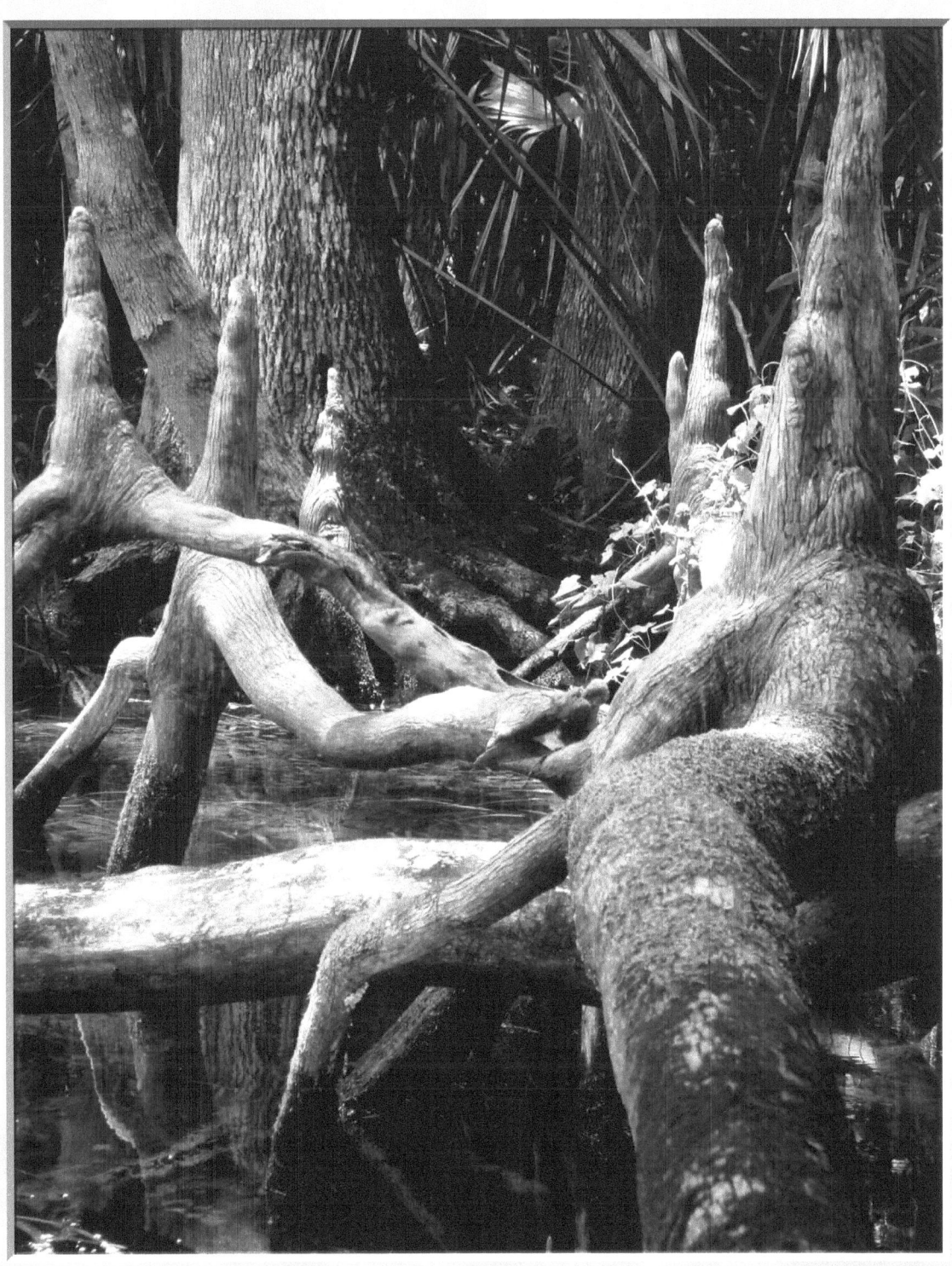

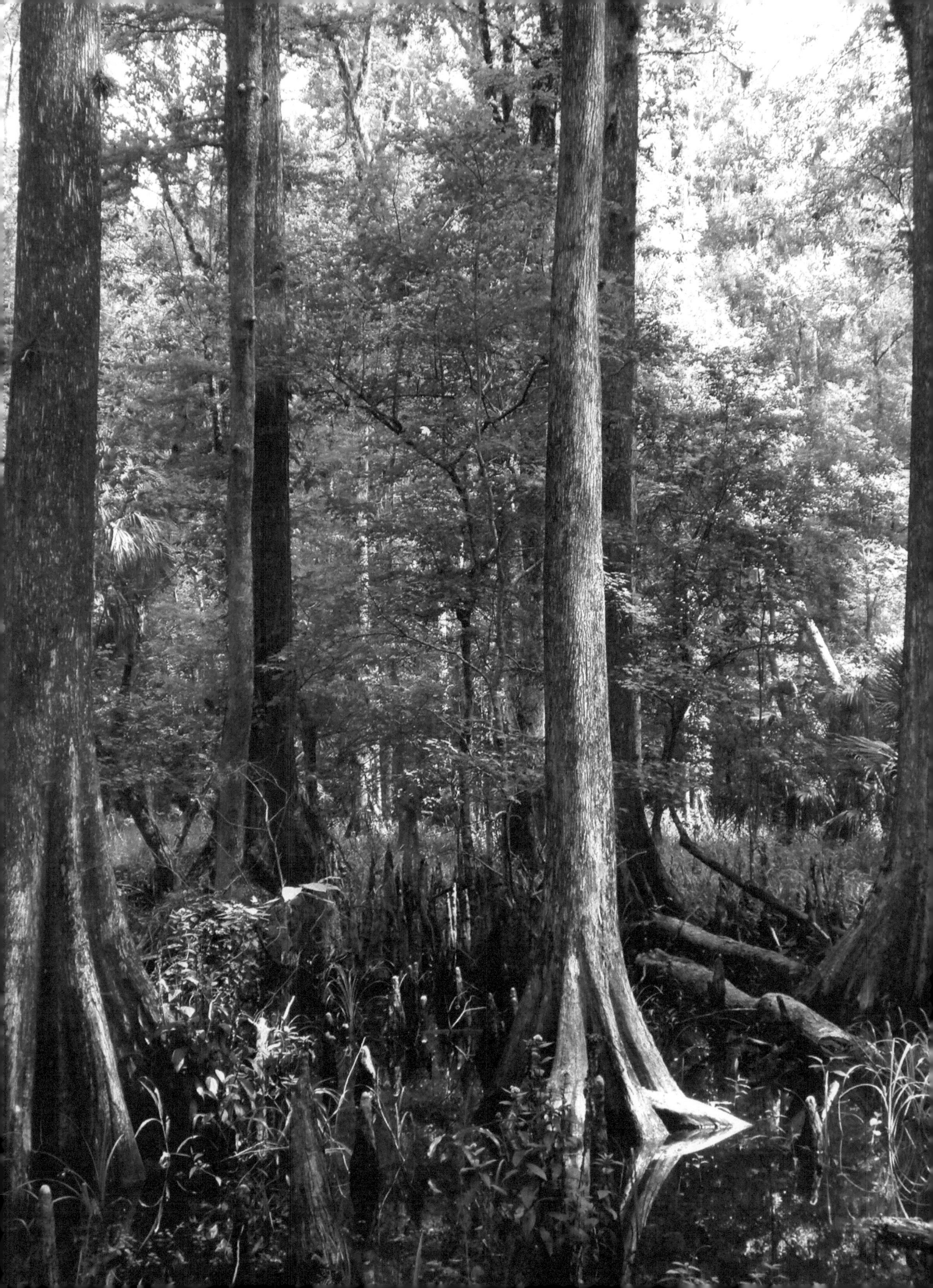

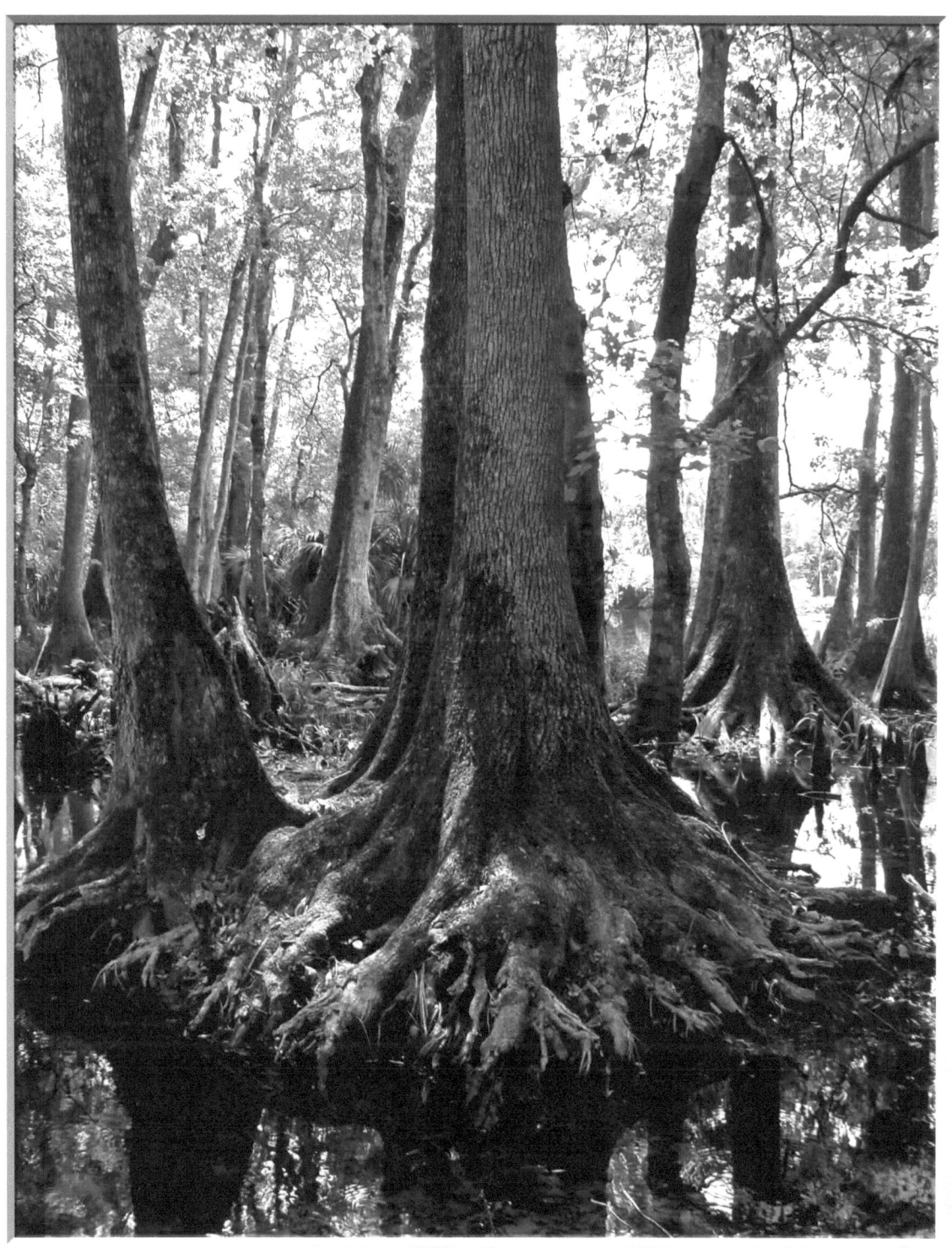

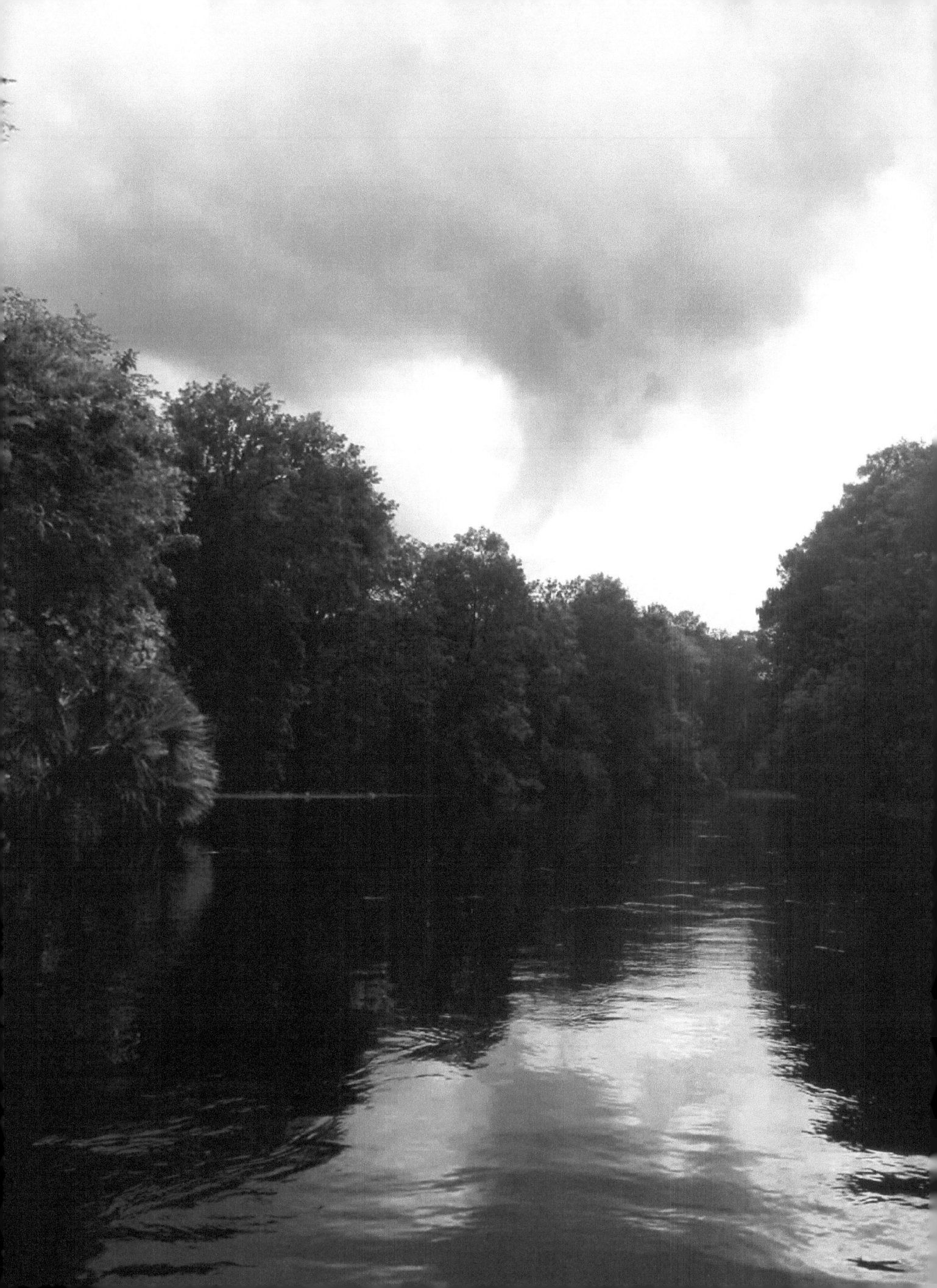

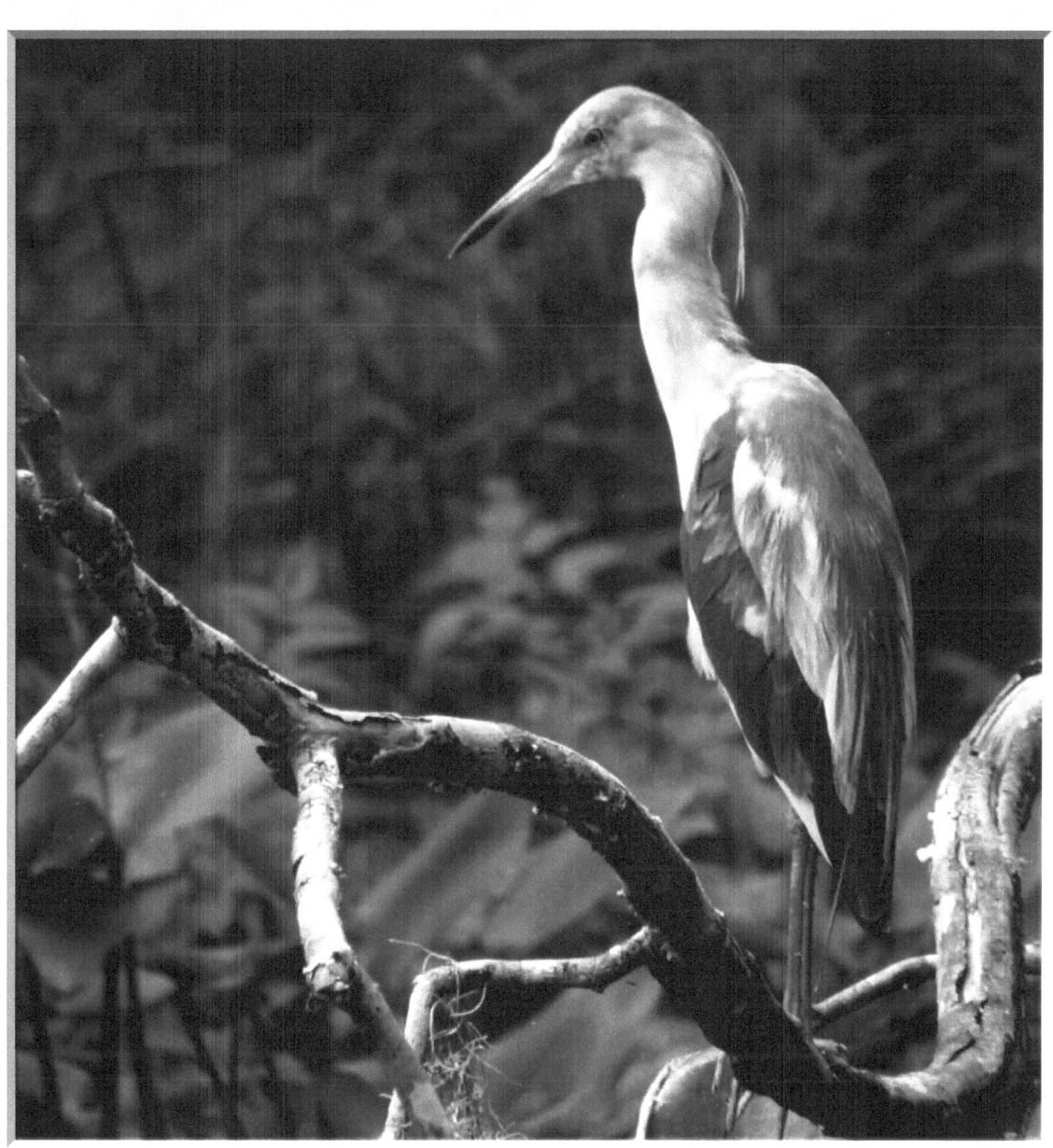

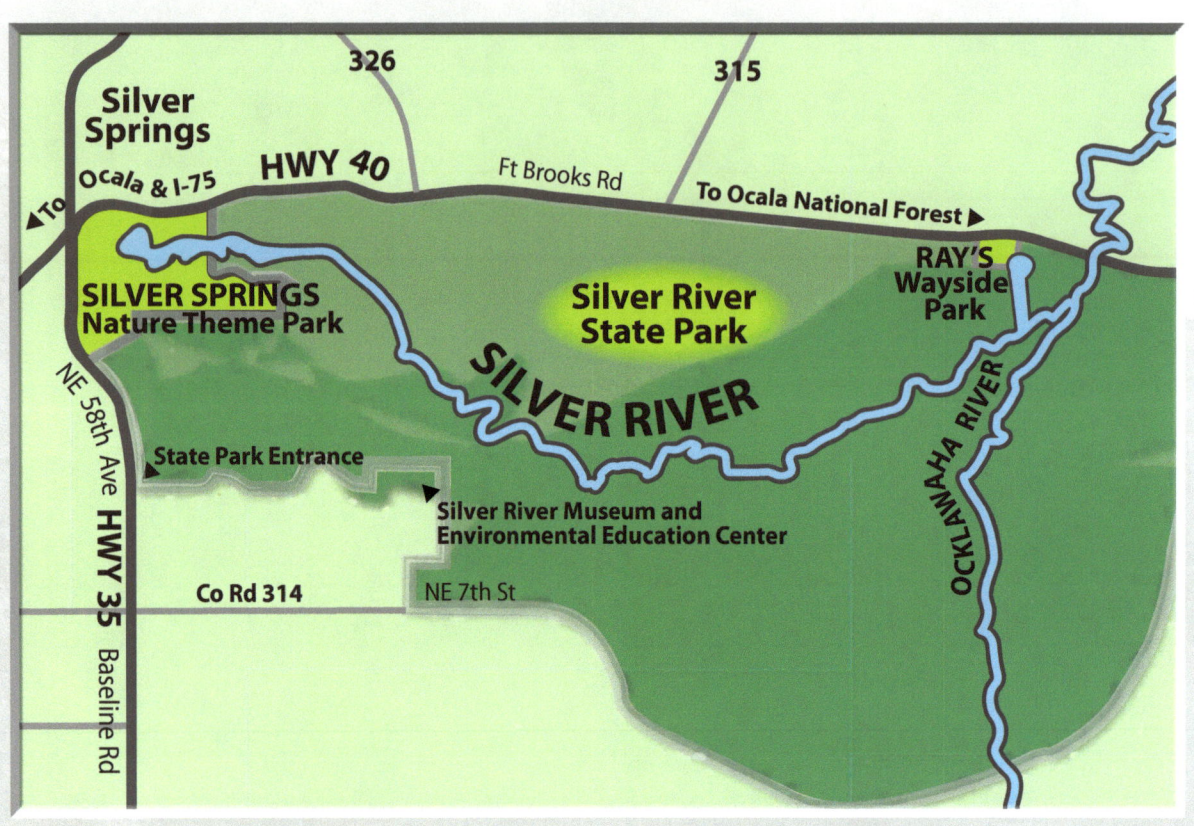

Ray's Wayside Park: 9560 NE 28th Lane (Hwy 40), Silver Springs, Florida

Silver River State Park: One mile south of Hwy 40 on State Road 35

Silver Springs Nature Theme Park: 5656 East Silver Springs Blvd. (Hwy 40)